Infusing Vocabulary Into the Reading–Writing Workshop

Learn how to make vocabulary instruction more effective by making better use of mini-lessons and word study time to achieve durable learning about words and how they work. In this essential new book, literacy expert Amy Benjamin presents her 4E model (Exposure, Exploration, Engagement, Energy) for teaching vocabulary so that students gain deep understanding, improving their overall language and literacy skills. Benjamin guides you through bringing these 4Es to life in your K–8 reading–writing workshop.

♦ Exposure: Enrich your teacher talk with sophisticated words and phrases to facilitate natural language acquisition and application of new words.
♦ Exploration: Promote consistent vocabulary growth with a multifaceted instructional approach that incorporates etymology, word associations, word families, spelling, and morphology.
♦ Engagement: Build students' confidence by encouraging meaningful use of new words, both in and out of the classroom.
♦ Energy: Enliven your workshop and increase participation with a variety of word games, puzzles, projects, and cooperative learning activities.

Each chapter provides practical examples and scenarios to help you apply the model to your own classroom. The appendices include a variety of strategies for organizing reading–writing workshops, a thorough introduction to academic word lists and their role in vocabulary instruction, and an analysis of forty Latin and Greek word roots for mini-lessons.

Amy Benjamin is a national education consultant and author of twelve books on teaching literacy, including *Infusing Grammar Into the Writer's Workshop* with Barbara Golub. Before becoming a consultant, she was an award-winning English teacher in Montrose, New York.

Infusing Vocabulary Into the Reading–Writing Workshop

A Guide for Teachers in Grades K–8

Amy Benjamin

Routledge
Taylor & Francis Group

NEW YORK AND LONDON

First published 2017
by Routledge
711 Third Avenue, New York, NY 10017

and by Routledge
2 Park Square, Milton Park, Abingdon, Oxon, OX14 4RN

Routledge is an imprint of the Taylor & Francis Group, an informa business

© 2017 Taylor & Francis

Library of Congress Cataloging-in-Publication Data
A catalog record for this book has been requested

ISBN: 978-1-138-12613-8 (hbk)
ISBN: 978-1-138-12614-5 (pbk)
ISBN: 978-1-315-64706-7 (ebk)

Typeset in Palatino
by Apex CoVantage, LLC

Contents

Meet the Author

After enjoying a long and rewarding career as an English teacher in the Hendrick Hudson School District in Montrose, New York, **Amy Benjamin** now works as a national and international consultant. Her goal is to improve education by helping teachers recognize the role that language plays in learning. As such, the Common Core State Standards, with their emphasis on literacy as a foundational skill across all subject areas, fit perfectly into her vision of education reform. Amy has been honored for excellence in teaching by Tufts University, Union College, and the New York State English Council. Her classroom was used as a model for standards-based teaching by the New York State Education Department. Amy lives in Dutchess County, New York, with her husband, Howard. Their son, Mitchell, lives in California and works in the television industry. This is the fourteenth book that she has written for Eye On Education. Find out more about Amy's work and download resources at www.amybenjamin.com.

Introduction: The *Why* and the *How*

Ideas are preserved and communicated by means of words. It necessarily follows that we cannot improve the language of any science, without at the same time improving the science itself; neither can we, on the other hand, improve a science without improving the language or nomenclature which belongs to it.

Antoine-Laurent Lavoisier, *Elements of Chemistry*, 1790

Picture this: Monday: "Please open your vocabulary workbooks to Unit 7." The fourth graders meet this week's list of twenty "grade level" words, as selected by the authors of this particular vocabulary series. The students go about their Monday routine of looking each word up in the dictionary (not necessarily a dictionary that is appropriate for fourth graders). They write down the definition (the shortest one will do fine) and use the word in a sentence (a sentence that does not change the form of the word as it appears on the list). This activity takes about fifteen minutes of class time, with the expectation that students will "finish" the twenty words for homework. On Tuesday, there will be a spelling pretest, as the vocabulary list doubles as a spelling list for the week. Tuesday's homework will be to check their spelling against the list in the workbook and to write each misspelled word five times. On Wednesday, ten minutes of class time is allotted to starting the fill-in-the-blank exercises in the workbook, finishing them for homework. Thursday is word-find puzzle day, as a means of reviewing the spelling.

Thursday's homework is to study for Friday's quiz, which, this week, will consist of a matching column—words on the left, brief definitions on the right. Turn the page and it's Monday again, with twenty more words marching in. The workbook has thirty units, interspersed with "cumulative reviews" every fourth chapter. Rinse. Repeat. Vocabulary should grow by some 600 words by the end of fourth grade.

Picture this: The teacher enacts the same procedures as just described, the only difference being that the words are drawn from literature that is currently being read as a whole class. The word list may be presented before, during, or after the reading has been done, depending on the philosophy of the teacher.

Picture this: In a workshop classroom, during read-aloud time, the teacher stops at certain points in the reading to ask students what word they think comes next. She does this when the word in question is one that the students probably do not know, but the context suggests a word that they probably *do* know—a synonym for the targeted word. Now, when she reads the whole sentence, the targeted (new) word will make sense. She might use the Big Book or document camera to direct attention to the words before and after (context), or to a picture on the page. She might ask leading questions to elicit the meaning of an unknown word. She might ask the students to act out the sentence, in an attempt to ascertain the meaning of an unknown word. She might say the meaning of the unknown word and quickly move on. During conference time, she might suggest a few "more interesting" words in a child's in-progress writing piece.

In the preceding three models, vocabulary is being addressed. Surely, students will have picked up a few words from these efforts. But the disadvantages are that "a few words" are not enough when you consider (1) the importance of vocabulary in reading, writing, and thinking; (2) the deficits in vocabulary knowledge and skills that your students probably have; and (3) how simple it would be to upgrade into vocabulary instruction that actually does increase the number of words that students know and use and the word-learning skills that will help them learn thousands of words that will not be explicitly taught.

The missed opportunities of all three models can be expressed in two words: *shallow processing*. It isn't that you can't improve vocabulary by using a workbook or by selecting words in context from literature. If you operate in a reading–writing workshop that supplements instruction with traditional resources, I would not tell you to throw away your workbooks and literature-based vocabulary lists, unless you want to. I am saying that you need to select the words more deliberately, explain words more deeply, and provide more experiences with the words so that they nestle into your students' minds and lives and stay there.

Vocabulary and the Common Core Standards

One of the reasons why the Common Core Standards for English Language Arts and Literacy specify and emphasize the need for vocabulary instruction (both explicit and implicit) is that vocabulary instruction has been given insufficient attention, particularly in the primary grades. One of the major shifts in instruction and focus stipulated by the Standards regards academic vocabulary: "Students constantly build the transferable vocabulary they need to access grade level complex texts" (National Governors Association Center for Best Practices, Council of Chief State School Officers, 2010). The ability to read and write about complex text and vocabulary knowledge share a symbiotic relationship: although efforts to comprehend text that is above a reader's comfort level will grow vocabulary, the reader does have to enter challenging text with sufficient vocabulary for comprehension to happen in the first place. So vocabulary knowledge is necessary for comprehension, and comprehension is also necessary to grow vocabulary.

Despite the many commendable qualities of reading–writing workshop (student motivation and engagement in literacy activities; routinizing positive reading and writing habits; structures that foster differentiation, data collection, and formative assessment), it doesn't really address vocabulary growth systematically or thoroughly, *so we have to fix that.* If I were to describe the way vocabulary is often taught, some words I might use would be *marginalized, limited,* and *disorganized.* And if I were to describe the way vocabulary needs to be taught so that it results in durable growth, I would use the words *rich, gradual, cumulative, recursive, aggressive, purposeful, pervasive,* and *organized.*

No one argues against the importance of vocabulary knowledge. Clear and consistent research "shows a strong relationship between vocabulary size and reading comprehension level; moreover, that relationship grows stronger as students progress through school" (Snow et al., 2007, as quoted in David, 2010). But there is plenty of argument about how vocabulary is best taught: Is vocabulary something that is "caught not taught" as a by-product of reading? Yes and no. Yes, a reader of texts that contain unfamiliar vocabulary will pick up words at a slow but decidedly steady pace. But, no, that pace is not fast *enough* to meet the demands, and if the text lacks challenging vocabulary, there will be little to be learned. Expecting that an already poor reader is going to advance her vocabulary by reading books with challenging vocabulary is a negative feedback loop, like expecting a poor person to start a lucrative business without a loan. (It is also something akin to the fact that those most in need of financial assistance get the stiffest interest rates on the least amount of money.) Explicit instruction on well-chosen words and about word components must fortify the curriculum, whether it's reading–writing workshop or not.

But that explicit instruction must be effective, and too often, it is not. And when it is not (which is usually), we educators tend to dismiss the whole idea of vocabulary instruction, rather than trade in what we have (that isn't working) for a better way. In *Teaching Vocabulary to Improve Reading Comprehension*, William E. Nagy (1988) posits that there are two reasons why vocabulary instruction has failed to increase reading comprehension. The first is the shallow processing that is done with traditional methods. Reading comprehension is the real game. Let's say it's ice hockey. If your practice puck has been a balloon and your stick has been a fly swatter, don't expect any miracles on ice. But that doesn't mean you shouldn't practice. It means you have to do a better job matching your practice to the game.

Nagy's second explanation for the unreliable cause and effect between vocabulary instruction (even if it's pretty good) and reading comprehension is the mismatch between words that are taught and words that are read in a given text. And that gate swings both ways, because a reader does not have to know every word in a text in order to comprehend it. So, we may be spending a great deal of time teaching vocabulary—time that could be used having the children reading—and the words we've taught may even have been learned, but, still, there is little reward for a text having none of our new words. This is what I'm calling the "spit-in-the-ocean" principle. It goes like this:

> So many words, so little time. And if I were to spend the amount of time needed to teach all of the words my students don't know in the texts they are reading, we would not have time to read, and they would lose the benefits of reading.

Nagy (1988) says:

> At this point, one might draw the conclusion that effective vocabulary instruction for comprehension would require the teachers to devote absurdly large amounts of time and energy to vocabulary instruction. They would have to cover every word in the selection that students might not know with rich, intensive instruction that ties the words in with background knowledge, engaging the students actively in meaningful processing.
>
> (29)

So, teachers (and schools, and curriculum writers) give up where they shouldn't because even though the sheer number of unknown words in a text may preclude us from teaching all of them thoroughly, the readers do not need to know all of those words for sufficient comprehension anyway. Not every word is essential to meaning. Written and oral language supplies redundancies, examples, and explanations that help us even if we stumble over as many as 10% of the words in some texts.

Given the importance of vocabulary knowledge and the deficits we recognize in our students, *and* given the need to take great care in how we use our time, we need to make wise decisions that will allow us to have it both ways: extensive, engaging reading and explicit (also engaging) vocabulary instruction.

> The teacher's goal must therefore be to find the optimal division of labor between incidental learning and explicit vocabulary instruction—to know how much time and energy to spend on teaching word meanings and how much to depend on the students' ability to learn on their own.
>
> (Nagy, 1988, 32–33)

The beauty of reading–writing workshop is that it gives much leeway to teachers to make student-based decisions. "The key issue is to identify the specific type of difficulties posed by different words in the text and to adapt instruction (a reading–writing workshop specialty!) to deal efficiently with them" (Nagy, 1988, 33).

Regarding vocabulary, reading–writing workshop relies heavily on the use of context clues, but context clues are not always reliable or even present. In his seminal study on vocabulary instruction, *Teaching Vocabulary to Improve Reading Comprehension* (1988), William E. Nagy explains the mistake we make when we place too much faith in the power of context clues: "Most contexts in normal text are relatively uninformative. The context around any unfamiliar word tells us something about its meaning, but very seldom does any single context give very complete information" (6). According to a study by Jenkins et al. (1984, quoted in Marzano, 2004), "to learn a word requires anywhere from 6 to 10 exposures to the word in context" (67).

It makes sense for teachers to provide brief definitions during an oral reading and then quickly move on, but that is not a substitute for vocabulary *instruction*. Those flash-in-the-pan definitions serve a momentary purpose in keeping the story moving, and that's important, but hearing a brief definition does not result in durable learning. Being able to recite a definition is called declarative knowledge, knowledge of a fact. Thinking that someone knows a word based on the ability to recite or match a definition is like thinking we know a person because we know his name. True knowledge of a word takes time, involves more than parroting a memorized definition, and is akin to knowing how to use a tool for its intended purpose and even for an improvised purpose. There's a name for that kind of knowledge: we call it procedural knowledge, and gaining it is often done unconsciously, in the course of doing something else. Blaine Ray, an expert in foreign language teaching through a technique that involves kinesthetic learning and storytelling, says that learning a word is something that happens to you, rather than something you consciously do. Our job is to learn how to make lots of words happen to students every day, using the various opportunities available in reading–writing workshop.

Frequent, purposeful, and broad reading improves vocabulary considerably, and workshop teachers are correct in believing that their approach connects vocabulary growth to the large amount of reading that children do in class, as well as the reading that they will supposedly do on their own as a result of cultivating a love of reading for pleasure. However, serious studies, such as those done and/or cited by Nagy and Marzano (see bibliographies in this volume), illuminate the need for a level of vocabulary growth that not only exceeds that which can be gained from reading alone, but also teaches word-learning skills, particularly how to trace Latin and Greek morphemes.

Let's consider for a moment the relationship between reading and vocabulary from two angles: first, how vocabulary knowledge enables reading comprehension; and then, how reading with comprehension grows vocabulary. "The proportion of difficult words in a text is the single most powerful predictor of text difficulty, and a reader's general vocabulary knowledge is the single best predictor of how well that reader can understand text" (Anderson and Freebody, 1981, as quoted in Nagy, 1988, p. 1). All readability formulas take vocabulary into account. The simple ones consider only the length of the words. More sophisticated measurements include the rarity of the words, the number of times words are repeated within a text, and the number of words referring to abstract concepts. As a rule of thumb, a reader needs to know about 95% of the words in a text for adequate comprehension (Hirsh and Nation, 1992). A reader who knows fewer than 95% of the words will likely be impeded by lack of fluency (having enough speed to keep up with the flow of information) and lack of overall comprehension. But skillful, well-instructed readers have tools to hoist themselves up to the 95% word knowledge level while reading a text. In *addition* to using context clues, skillful readers deploy tools that enable recognition of word components (affixes and morphology), cognates, grammatical inflections, and syllabication, thereby making educated guesses about unfamiliar multisyllabic words. We'll be calling such strategies *word attack skills*. True word attack skills go beyond the mere "sounding out" of words: they have to do with putting meaning together based on word parts *and* context.

Now let's think about the reverse: How does the act of reading build vocabulary? As already mentioned, here is where commonly held assumptions about the extent to which vocabulary grows by reading alone need to be challenged (and have been challenged for some thirty-plus years, actually). William E. Nagy (quoted in *Building Background Knowledge for Academic Achievement*; Marzano, 2004) did the math:

> If students spend 25 minutes a day reading at a rate of 200 words per minute for 200 days, they will read a million words of text annually and encounter between 15,000 and 30,000 unfamiliar words. If they learn 1 in 20 of these words, their yearly gain in vocabulary will be between 750 and 1,500 words.

(63)

Sounds like a lot! But when you dig deeper into not only the number of words but also the kinds of words that students need to learn for academic success, you see the need for explicit instruction in words that have been selected for their academic utility.

For one thing, the number of words learned through reading, as previously outlined, depends on the level of text difficulty for a particular student. It stands to reason that if a student is reading text in which she already knows all the words, she is not going to learn any new ones as a result of the time spent reading. (Granted, she may well learn new uses for familiar words and gain other benefits, in terms of background knowledge, that will facilitate her learning words through contexts in *other* texts.)

Furthermore, the new words gleaned from reading may come from a narrow field, such as horseback riding or playing hockey. These technical words may not be relevant to the nuts-and-bolts discourse of academic text.

And the pace of learning words through context, not only is slow, albeit steady, but also varies depending on the number of words that the reader already knows: "A high-ability student has a 19 percent chance of learning a new word in context, whereas a low-ability student has an 8 percent chance" (Swinborn and de Glopper, quoted in Marzano, 2004, 67). Accordingly, the younger the student is, the less likely it is that she will learn a new word from context alone. For high school students, reading has a bigger page-per-page payoff in new words learned, provided that the text contains unknown words in rich contexts.

All of this is not to say that, in the best of worlds and workshops—where students are reading a lot, and widely—explicit (a.k.a. direct) instruction *is still necessary*. Besides being necessary for a full education, explicit instruction on well-chosen words is also measurable, controllable, and teachable through various means. However, "the reality of the classroom is that teachers are generally not familiar and not comfortable with anything more than dictionary definitions and the use of sentence context to teach vocabulary" (Berne and Blachowicz, 2008–2009 in Rasinski et al., 2011, 1). This book meets that need.

To summarize: the three most relied-upon methods of growing vocabulary as currently practiced in reading–writing workshops are (1) using context clues, (2) hearing brief definitions during a read-aloud, and (3) reading frequently. While all of these practices need to continue, they need to be supplemented and fortified by deep word study, the kind of word study that involves spending quality time with words through explicit instruction. In the words of police chief Martin Brody, "You're gonna need a bigger boat."

Now picture this: During a read-aloud of *Matilda* by Roald Dahl, the teacher stops at the end of this sentence, asking the children to guess the word that comes next: " 'You ignorant little slug,' the Trunchbull _____." The children can easily come up with *yelled*, *hollered*, *screamed*, *shouted*, and even *screeched* and *scolded*. But none of them say the word that was the author's choice: *bellowed*. This is a new word, but a word whose meaning is already understood. As a synonym for the words that mean *speaking loudly and strongly*, the word *bellow* already has a designated meaning in the children's mental closets. The teacher, having prepared for this teachable moment, shows a picture of fire bellows, an unfamiliar tool, as these particular students do not live in homes with fireplaces. In less than a minute, she explains that, like the human voice, fire bellows transform a concentrated gust of air into a powerful force.

Now picture this: Students are learning about animal habitats. They have been assigned to various informational texts matched to their reading levels (guided reading). As a mini-lesson, the teacher uses a visual having three columns: Column 1: picture and name of an animal; Column 2: picture of its habitat; Column 3: the name of the habitat. Words for habitats are listed in scrambled order on the board, and then moved into place. There are only five to seven words per day for a week, but each day's word list contains at least one word from the day before. The words for the week are: *wetlands*, *desert*, *tundra*, *prairie*, *tropical rain forest*, *temperate forest*, *taiga mountains*, *burrow*, *aerie*, *polar region*, *freshwater*, *coral reef*.

Now picture this: At a word study station, students play online vocabulary games and puzzles. These games recruit knowledge not only about meaning, but also about word forms, word components, and spelling.

Now picture this: During conference time, the teacher suggests and briefly explains one or two words as she jots them down. These are words that would fit well in the piece of writing that the child is working on, but are a stretch.

Now picture this: As a mid-workshop interruption, the teacher reminds the students that they should be using at least one word that they have never used before. She takes a moment to have students call out their "brand-new-for-me" words, asking them to briefly say what they mean.

Now picture this: As a mini-lesson, the teacher routinizes "Latin root of the week" once a month. This week's Latin root is *-tract*. Over the course of a week, she does the following: She writes the words *detract* and *distract* on the board, and uses them in a rich, illustrative context. Students do a think-pair-share to hypothesize the meaning of the root *-tract*. She draws a "word tree," whose branches include words that derive from the root *-tract*. Some of these words are probably known to the students; others are probably unknown: *attract, subtract, retract, tractor, traction, abstract, contract, extract, protract*. She gives very brief definitions and rich contexts for these words, and asks the students to do a think-pair-share about what they think the meaning of the root *-tract* is, based on what all of these words have in common. Working in small groups, the students hypothesize the meanings of three of the words (each group having a different three words) and then use their dictionary skills to check themselves. Their dictionary skills include looking at the etymological information, which appears at the end of each entry. Throughout the week, the teacher is careful to include words with the root *-tract* (as well as previously learned words with Latin roots) in classroom language. This means that she uses targeted words in her own speech, shows how their use would be relevant in everyday writing, and points out words with the targeted root in classroom readings.

Are all of these efforts worth the time? If there is anything more important—academically—than vocabulary growth, I don't know what it would be. The mind does not use words only to communicate. The purpose of words, primarily, is to access concepts. Lacking an adequate vocabulary for communicating and thinking, our minds are like a teenager's closet: we have to dig through all kinds of crumpled up, rolled up wads of something or other to find what we may or may not have, and when we do find it, it isn't exactly ready to go. Compare this to the proud owner of a meticulously arranged, color-coded, and well-stocked closet. Not only can we find what we need, but all of the accessories are right there where we need them. An ample, deep vocabulary allows us to access the tools for thinking—words, words, words!

But, with everything else screaming for attention in our literacy block— why can't "fancy" words wait until high school? There's a very good reason why they can't. "Catch-up," in education, is a losing proposition. We simply haven't figured out a way to make up for lost time, and we never will, because the demands of schooling keep increasing from grade to grade, leaving widening gaps between the haves and the have-nots, vocabulary-wise. Vocabulary deficits are not just *vocabulary* deficits. They make it impossible to learn at the same rate as those who have adequate vocabularies. "Vocabulary size is a convenient proxy for a whole range of educational attainments and abilities—not just skill in reading, writing, listening, and speaking, but also general knowledge of science, history, and the arts" (Hirsch, 2013, 3). The effects of early schooling in vocabulary (pre-school, in fact) are not immediately apparent. They show up in the mid-elementary grades when the language becomes more abstract. When we have full control of a word, we have more than just that one word: as far as the brain is concerned, a word is a "packet" of information, easily retrievable. While short-term memory can handle only seven individual bits of information, knowledge of a word that represents an abstract concept (as our academic words do) consolidates information, giving us more wattage in short-term memory.

But getting back to why vocabulary instruction can't wait:

It's important to grasp the extreme difficulty of narrowing the verbal gap between advantaged and disadvantaged students. The problem has been called the Matthew Effect, an allusion to Matthew 25:29: "For unto every one that hath shall be given, and he shall have abundance: but from him that hath not shall be taken away even that which he hath." Advantaged students who arrive in the classroom with background knowledge and vocabulary will understand what a textbook or teacher is saying and will therefore learn more; disadvantaged students who lack such prior knowledge will fail to understand and thus fall even further behind, relative to their fellow students.

(Hirsch, 2013, 11)

The secret sauce is to repair vocabulary gaps early, *before* they affect learning in the later grades.

Vocabulary instruction—explicit and implicit—has to be ongoing, aggressive, pervasive, recursive, and planned. But happily, the best vocabulary instruction—that which adheres to the tenets of natural language acquisition—is joyfully easy to accomplish if we just remember how words get learned and stay learned. Think of toddlers. The way they learn words through natural language acquisition is exactly the way they will always learn words throughout their lives. I think vocabulary growth can be accomplished through the interaction of what we are calling the 4Es: Exposure, Exploration, Engagement, Energy.

Four Es

Exposure: Every word that finds its "forever home" in our brains ("productive vocabulary," or words that come out of our own mouths and hands) gets there because of repeated exposure in the course of meaningful communication ("receptive vocabulary," or words that come into our ears and eyes). The richer the context in which a new word nestles, the greater the information that can be picked up about the word. New words need to be heard and seen in a variety of contexts *and* a variety of forms. And bombardment with lots of exposure all at once won't work: The human mind needs processing time, exposure over time. Think of how long it takes you to learn the names of your students in a new semester. It probably takes you several days, at least. Going over their names again and again on the first day of school will not guarantee that you will learn them. You learn them over time, as you distinguish one student from another from day to day.

Words Learned "from Underneath"

Picture a pond covered with lily pads, on top of which lie beaded-up water droplets. Lily pads have what botanists call hydrophobic properties, which means that they repel water. Yet, lily pads produce lush flowers, water lilies that surely absorb sufficient water. The surface of the lily pads and their showy flowers are the very symbol of calmness and simple beauty. Ah, but underneath is another story! You might be surprised at the radii of arteries that branch out on the underside of a lily pad, home to various and sundry creatures and their eggs: snails, beetles, damselflies, mites, and even sponges. A forest of well-nourished stalks sways below, surrounded by gliding fish and turtles. The water underneath the surface teems with unseen life that nourishes the lily pad and its flowers even while those beaded-up drops that you can see either evaporate or dissipate into the muck, there to become useful.

Such it is with the words we teach. We may be dropping words on the surface. Some of those words may end up being absorbed. Most just look pretty until they disappear. It's the pervasive, underneath action that creates durable growth.

Exploration: Words have depth. We need to exceed brief definitions of words. To really understand and remember a word, we need to spend some quality time with it, get to know its history and family (etymology), subtleties, synonyms, near-synonyms, antonyms, near-antonyms, spelling, and morphological forms. I say: never teach just one word. Always use the targeted word to reinforce the meaning of related words as well as awareness about words in general: how they derive from roots, for example, how they differ ever so slightly from synonyms, even how their spelling gives up clues to their meaning. I think of a word as a little archeological specimen, amenable to exploration and discovery about the world in which it lives now and the years and spaces over which it has lived.

To explore a word is to exceed a brief definition. Many of the words we teach represent abstract concepts. Abstractions are understood through concretions; hence the importance of examples and visuals in teaching a word. Most of the words in your own vocabulary that represent abstract concepts got there not because you were taught a definition but because you attached examples of the concept to the word for it. Examples allow for visualization, association, and something called "concept attainment," which is the carving out of features for a concept.

Engagement: As you will read in Chapter 3, engagement means more than just being busy and compliant. The kind of engagement with vocabulary we are looking for involves personal investment, rigor, curiosity, risk, and inquiry. Because language is social, we want students to work together as much as possible, and we want to hear their newly learned words buzzing around the room as they speak with each other as well as to us, and we to them.

The Glossary of Education Reform (edglossary.org/student-engagement) delineates six different kinds of engagement:

Intellectual engagement is increased when students have choices and challenges that mean something to them. Because learning is the result of problem-solving, we need to engage students in vocabulary lessons that are more than just having them hear or look up a definition of a word that we told them to learn.

Emotional engagement is increased when students work together in a positive way. Vocabulary learning should be joyful and social. Experts in language acquisition speak of the importance of having a *low affective filter*, which means that learning is impeded by negative emotions. Vocabulary learning should never be considered boring by the learner or the teacher. While we differ in the kinds of activities that we think are boring, one thing is sure: the brain pays little attention to that which we find boring.

Behavioral engagement happens best when classroom routines are clear and the teacher has effective ways of redirecting attention. The disengaged class can be easier to manage than a class full of children who are excited. There's always a balance to be sought between routines that establish a comforting sense of organization and predictability and those that flatten into a dreary monotony. A well-operating reading–writing workshop has a variety of groupings among students and a variety of tasks that, ideally, result in students knowing what to do and how to transition between activities.

Physical engagement, or kinesthetic learning, is often used to teach verbs and adverbs, as students act out actions and manners of actions. Physical engagement also refers to students holding their bodies in a manner that is conducive to learning. In a workshop classroom, there are times when children are sitting in a circle on a comfy rug, reading on beanbag chairs, sitting in the rocking chair, and so on.

Social engagement refers to the interactions among students and between students and teachers. This is where the reading–writing workshop is particularly strong, as students work as a class community in various configurations. Communication and collaboration is at the heart of the reading–writing workshop.

Cultural engagement happens when all students feel that their languages, backgrounds, families, accents, religions, and customs are honored. This is especially important for our newly arrived immigrants and those whose home language is not English.

Energy: Very few children ever think it is fun to look up words in a dictionary, copy definitions, fill in blanks on a worksheet, use the words in a sentence, drill the words on flashcards, study for a test, and take the test. So what? Not everything has to be fun. Some things in life are hard, miserable, painful, and boring. Get used to it, kid. No more baby stuff. You're in fourth grade now.

We humans simply dismiss and forget information learned through boring activities. The good news is that humans love wordplay, games, discovery, and socializing. And everyone feels smarter when they learn a new word, even smarter when they actually use one! So, bust out the word games, puzzles, fun projects, and cooperative learning activities. A good vocabulary lesson or center is lively, social, noisy, and enthusiastic. This is not only because fun is motivational. It is also because that which we learn joyfully is most likely to be retained.

Now let's consider the first word in the title of this book: *infusing*. I've used that word quite deliberately because to infuse is to fill, to color the entirety of something by getting into every part of it, the way tea leaves infuse hot water, transforming it into tea.

> Infusion is based on the idea that children's vocabulary is built through multiple exposures to words in multiple contexts. . . . It is a purposeful approach in which the teacher seeks to incorporate "incidental" exposure to target words throughout the day.
>
> (Kindle, 2011, 12)

The infusion of vocabulary into the reading–writing workshop has a strong element of intentionality: the teacher's actions are strongly informed by the principles of natural language acquisition, which will allow for the gradual but durable learning of words to which humans are repeatedly exposed in rich contexts. While it is true and important to know about the process through which humans glean words in the course of communication, it is also true and important to understand effective ways of teaching wisely selected words explicitly.

Exposure, Exploration, Engagement, Energy: It's easier than you might think if you use elevated, academic language in the course of what comes naturally in communicating as a teacher. In the coming chapters, we'll look at each of these 4 Es in detail, showing how they can be absorbed right into your existing balanced literacy block. If you need a refresher on what balanced literacy is all about and how reading–writing workshop fits into it, please refer to Appendix A. Now let's dig into your 4Es, starting with the broadest and most pervasive one: *Exposure.*

Bibliography

Anderson, R.C. and P. Freebody. (1981). Vocabulary Knowledge: Comprehension and Teaching: Research Reviews. In J. Guthrie (Ed.), *Adolescents' Engagement in Academic Literacy* (pp. 77–117). Newark, DE: International Reading Association. Cited in Nagy, William E. (1988). *Teaching Vocabulary to Improve Reading Comprehension.* Urbana, IL: National Council of Teachers of English. 1.

Berne, Jennifer I. and Camille L.Z. Blachowicz. (December–January, 2008–2009). What reading teachers say about vocabulary instruction: Voices from the classroom. *The Reading Teacher*, 62(4), 314–323. International Literacy Association.

Dahl, Roald and Quentin Blake. (1988). *Matilda.* New York: Puffin Books. 29.

David, Jane L. (March 2010). *Educational Leadership.* Alexandria, VA: ASCD. Volume 67.

Foley, Joseph. (2004). *Language, Education and Discourse: Functional Approaches.* London: Continuum. 177.

Hirsch, E.D. (January 9, 2013). A wealth of words. *City Journal.* 3. The *Glossary of Education Reform: Edglossary.org/engagement.* Accessed June 10, 2016.

Hirsh, David and Paul Nation. (1992). What vocabulary size is needed to read unsimplified texts for pleasure. *Reading in a Foreign Language,* 8(2), 689–696. Available at http://nflrc.hawaii.edu/rfl/PastIssues/rfl82hirsh.pdf

Jenkins, Joseph R., Marcy L. Stein and Katherin Wysocki. (1984). *Learning Vocabulary through Reading: American Educational Research Journal.* Cited in Marzano, Robert J. (2004). *Building Background Knowledge for Academic Achievement.* Alexandria, VA: ASCD. 67.

Kindle, Karen J. (2011). *Using Read-Alouds to Teach Vocabulary.* New York: Scholastic. 12.

Marzano, Robert. (2004). *Building Background Knowledge for Academic Achievement.* Alexandria, VA: ASCD. 69.

Nagy, William E. (1988). *Teaching Vocabulary to Improve Reading Comprehension.* Urbana, IL: National Council of Teachers of English. 29.

National Governors Association Center for Best Practices, Council of Chief State School Officers. (2010). *Common Core State Standards: English Language Arts/Literacy Standards.* Washington, DC: National Governors Association. Retrieved from www.corestandards.org

Rasinski, Timothy, et al. (2011). *The Latin-Greek Vocabulary Connection: Building Elementary Students' Vocabulary Through Morphological Study.* Huntington Beach, CA: Teacher Created Materials Publishing. 1.

Ray, Blaine and Contee Seely. (2014). *Fluency Through TPR Storytelling: Achieving Real Language Acquisition in School,* Sixth Edition. Berkeley, California: Command Performance Language Institute. 7.

Snow, C.E., M.V. Porche, P.O. Tabors, and S.R. Harris. (2007). *Is Literacy Enough? PathWays to Academic Success for Adolescents.* Baltimore, MD: Paul H. Brookes. Cited in David, Jane L. (March 2010). *Educational Leadership.* Alexandria, VA: ASCD. Volume 67.

Swinborn, M.S.L. and K. de Glopper. (2002). Incidental word learning while reading: A meta-analysis. *Review of Educational Research,* 69(3), 261–285. Marzano, Robert J. (2004). *Building Background Knowledge for Academic Achievement.* Alexandria, VA: ASCD. 67.

1

Exposure

"I was absent yesterday. What did I miss?"

"We are taking our family on a week-long vacation. Can you please give us the work our daughter will be missing so she can do it while we are traveling?"

A student's learning experience in your class cannot be reduced to a packet of "work" to be "done." The exposure to repeated, multidimensional use of sophisticated words—words that the student is not exposed to outside of school—is arguably the most important element of education. It's irreplaceable, albeit invisible.

"We live in a sea of words," writes Steven A. Stahl in "How Words Are Learned Incrementally Over Multiple Exposures" (2003, 18). Words, in this metaphor, would be the fish in the sea. And there need to be a lot of them swimming around. Some fish cover territory; others remain in a niche. The sea of listening and reading (receptive language) needs to teem with fish of all kinds, for the stock to be replenished with speaking and writing (productive language). When fishermen catch a giant tuna, other smaller fish end up in the net. That is what we want to happen as we teach our targeted words explicitly: we pick up collateral words in the same net.

Don't be afraid to speak in an elevated way to the youngest of children.

A growing body of research and classroom practice show that building a sophisticated vocabulary at an early age is also key to raising reading success—and narrowing the achievement gap. Teachers are overcoming the age-old habit of speaking to young children in simplified language only. Instead, teachers who are conscious of natural language acquisition deliberately weave higher-level word choices into primary classrooms. Whether it's a discussion at morning meeting, informal talk at the block area, or a selection of read-aloud books, teachers are exposing younger children to language that, in many cases, exceeds the vocabulary level of a typical conversation between college graduates.

(Pappano, 2008, 1)

Any person can learn any word if that word is (1) used in a context having enough familiar words and concepts, and (2) repeated generously in the beginning stages and revisited over time.

When a word "settles in" to your brain, a bell does not ring to let you know. You may hear a word somewhere in your surroundings, just outside your consciousness. You pay attention to it on a subliminal level. You hear it again, this time in a different form. Maybe you notice it this time, but it fades, only to come into sharper focus the third time you hear it. The meaning of a word *emerges*, revealing more and more of itself with each context and form, until we use it correctly in several contexts and forms ourselves.

Learning words is not the same as learning, say, math. As a child learns math, she needs to build upon simpler, previously learned skills. First she learns to quantify (count), then to add, then to subtract. Learning to multiply depends upon understanding the concept of addition. Math is hierarchical. But learning words is not. You don't need to build up from commonly known words to learn rarer ones. The relative "difficulty" of a word is not related to its meaning, but to its frequency in the language in general and in a specific person's life and language experience. A child does not have to know or use the word *wait* before she can know and use the word *hesitate*. Nor is the word *hesitate* "more difficult" than the word *wait*. Once we understand that words are not learned developmentally, like math concepts, we understand that the sky's the limit for our students to learn any words, however long or rare. After all, word length is not an inherent obstacle to learning a word. If it were, children would never be able to learn German, a language that attaches adjectives to nouns, resulting in very long words. It happens to be that in English, the shorter words are usually more common than the longer ones, and hence more frequent. That is the only reason why short words are considered "easier" than long words in English. We happen to be exposed to short words earlier in life, and more frequently, than we are to longer words, and that is because of the history of the English language, which added Latinate and Greek-based words (which are multisyllabic) only after the base of the language had already been established by the Anglo-Saxons. It is a quirk of history that English has so many synonyms and that we happen to learn the shorter words before the longer ones.

A workshop classroom is a student-centered classroom. As such, it is even more critical that whatever language the teacher uses is infused with words that the students would not be using themselves and would probably not be hearing outside of school. Hearing academic, interesting, specific language is, all by itself, a good reason for going to school on a given day. It's not only what you are teaching that counts; it's how you say it that grows vocabulary incrementally. Insofar as you are capable of providing contextualized repeated exposure to words that your students would not have heard or seen otherwise, you *are* the curriculum, not just the person who presides over it.

Let's look at what happens when students are exposed to elevated discourse (by which, we mean teacher talk that is characterized by a steady flow of words that are new or partially known by students, when those words are surrounded by enough context to make them understandable). Dana A. Robertson and her colleagues (2014) cite studies that link "effective teacher talk" to:

- ◆ improved reading comprehension, which includes reading for enjoyment, strategic reading for targeted information, flexibility, and stamina
- ◆ improved ability to learn words from context, setting in motion a positive feedback loop
- ◆ improved ability to hold conversations with teachers, which includes asking, as well as answering, questions, both about content and about the learning process (metacognition)
- ◆ improved academic competency, which refers to not only having more knowledge, but also increasing capacity to learn, retain, and apply knowledge

When you think about the level of vocabulary that you use when speaking to your class, and when you think about how important it is for them to hear academic and specific language while in school, and when you think about the level of language that they are hearing outside of school, you will probably realize how much more you can do with your word choice in class.

A typical routine in your morning meetings might be to discuss the day's weather conditions. Even if you spend two to three minutes sharing the meteorology work (and call it *meteorology* work) you can make this a vocabulary-rich two to three minutes. Instead of having children report that it is *nice* outside, you can repeat these observations back to them with more sophisticated language. For example, *nice* can become *pleasant*. You can lift the level of this language over time, too. Perhaps *cloudy* becomes *overcast* and *sunny* becomes *clear*.

So now let's talk about what constitutes a teacher's "skillful use of talk." First of all, for words to be learned in context, the context itself, other than the targeted word, has to be already known. Sufficient context is known in the field of language acquisition as *comprehensible input*. If you've ever watched *Wheel of Fortune*, you've seen comprehensible input at work. As teachers, we should be using vocabulary that we suspect (or know) that our students don't quite know yet, but we surround the unknown word with comprehensible input. If speaking this way becomes a habit, then our students are fortunate: they will be learning words effortlessly.

Comprehensible input, also known as helpful context, can take many forms. Sometimes, we reword the targeted term immediately after we use it, as we did in the previous sentence.

We can provide examples, especially for abstract concepts. We can provide visuals, which can include photographs, cartoons, and movies. We can use physicality (bodies, faces, hands) to demonstrate a concept. We can tell stories that illustrate the concept. And, to help students make the leap from receptive to productive vocabulary, we can have them do any of the preceding themselves to demonstrate what they know.

Comprehensible input can also be achieved through showing where the targeted word fits in on a continuum of words for a given concept. For example, during accountable talk time, you may have students name the characteristics of a certain character. You can support students' articulation of their understanding by showing them how they can use specific language to describe characters. You can begin by creating a word ladder that describes just how deeply that character is stubborn, confused, compliant, naive, and so on. Let's look at Cherry Sue from Cynthia Rylant's *Poppleton* series. Students might describe Cherry Sue as "nosy." You can write this word toward the bottom of the word ladder. Adding a continuum of words from the bottom up, you might continue to show children other words that offer variations of the same idea; perhaps above *nosy* is the word *bothersome*, and then *irritating, obnoxious*, and so on. In this way, you are showing students not only how they can use specific words to describe their ideas, but also how they can use specific words to deepen their—and others'—understanding of the complexity of a text's characters. For example, suppose the concept is *I don't know what's going on*. We want to teach the word that would rightly fit into the frame: I'm _____. Suppose I think that most of the children in my class know the word *confused*. (If not, maybe they know the word *mixed-up* or *lost*.) I can use this comprehensible input as the teachable moment for words that express the concept of confusion in various kinds and degrees. To be a little confused is to be *unsure, uncertain, unclear, fuzzy,* or *foggy*. To be more than a little confused is to be *perplexed, befuddled,* or *disoriented*. To be seriously confused is to be *baffled,* or even *stupefied*. Then, there's a word that describes a combination of confusion and surprise: *dumbfounded!* or *thunderstruck!* Now, I don't expect my students to learn all of these words (all at once). I'm using the opportunity of creating an array of words around a given concept to provide comprehensible input about a targeted word and to introduce—at least touch briefly on—a few other words that students may encounter in their readings.

Words are absorbed over time. The term *spaced retrieval* refers to the reason why you don't learn and retain all of the names of your students the first time you take attendance on the first day of school. Spaced retrieval is a principle of vocabulary learning that guards against forgetting a word because not enough time has gone by to let it "sink in" to your brain. "Lots of repetitions in the early stages of learning are important so that the chances of learners remembering the words will be higher. That is, there is not enough time to forget" (Coxhead, 2006, 20). Words that just scamper along in rapid succession have a way of scampering out quickly, evading recapture. But words that are revisited over a bit of time have a way of telling the brain that they're here to stay. The brain makes neurological room for them. (Now would be a good time to point out that information that we take the time to think about—that is, reach into our brains for—tends to stay with us longer than easily gotten information. That is why it is better to try to dredge up a fact from our own internal search engines rather than reaching immediately for the nearest electronic device. Actually, the same is true for a quick lookup of a word in a dictionary rather than using brainpower to try to figure it out first.)

This Is Your Brain on Collocations

The human brain is an astonishing storage device. A person memorizes and organizes information automatically, as a by-product of exposure and engagement (we do not pay attention to boring things). And when we need information, the human brain knows how to deliver it in the form of words—not just a single word, but the word and its entourage.

There's a word for the concept that words tend to come in prefabricated units. We call it *collocation*. The brain stores words in units—collocations—because it's easier and more efficient to remember them that way. The instructional implication of this happy circumstance speaks to the importance of using targeted words authentically, in meaningful contexts, rather than in isolation. Because they have at least two parts, phrases may be easier to understand and remember than single words. Let's use the example of football jargon. A person knows the words *offensive, line,* and *offensive line.* Here's how it works in the brain: she has heard the individual words *offensive* and *line* far more than she has heard the unit *offensive line.* However, when she hears *offensive line,* that unit of meaning is easier to process than either of the two single words because of something called access points. *Offensive* is one access point in the brain; *line* is another. But the phrase *offensive line* becomes yet another access point, stored in the "football department" of the brain. Individual words, if they are associated with only one definition, can be found at one access point only. But collocations—words grouped together—can be accessed through their individual components (single words) *and also* through the phrase itself (Dabrowska, 18). Again, I'm raising this point in a chapter about exposure to emphasize the superiority of presenting words in authentic contexts rather than as items in a list.

Distributed practice: We've been talking about the difference between distributed practice (revisitation over a number of days and weeks) as opposed to massed practice (intensive visitation in a short period of time, such as a day or two). An important assumption about distributed practice is that, in providing exposure to a targeted word over time (revisiting it), we will be exposing students to the word in various contexts and forms. Let's say the word is *commit* for fourth grade. Full-scale distributed practice would entail hearing and seeing the word in grade-level contexts and forms (commit to a team, commit a crime, make a commitment, form a committee). While you could toss all of these examples out at once, and while it is a good idea to do so when teaching the word *commit* explicitly, you do need to be aware that it is only through re-exposure over time that the word has a fighting chance to stay learned.

Embedding words in rich, instructive contexts *on its own* (emphasis mine) did not contribute to better opportunities for vocabulary learning. It needed to be coupled with noticing and frequent meetings over a distributed period to improve vocabulary development. We have seen that vocabulary acquisition is indeed an incremental process, requiring multiple encounters with new or partially known words in a wide range of tasks.

(Joe, 2010)

Now let's talk about drill. Drill is a kind of exposure, and perhaps it has its place when used sparingly and with awareness of its limitations. But drill alone is not to be considered sufficient exposure, and that is because of the shallowness of processing provided by drill.

Using the word *drill* to mean rote repetition is a misleading metaphor. Actual drills allow you to break resistant ground and then go deep. Classroom drills just graze the surface, and do so repeatedly. Although a classroom drill may result in memorizing information, it won't result in broadening and deepening knowledge about a word. It won't illuminate subtle meanings, present varied forms, or extract the word components that will lead to learning words sharing similar structures. And by drill, we also mean the use of flashcards. (In Chapter 4, we'll suggest some ways in which flashcards and drill-like repetitive games can be used more productively.)

Just how many times do you need to hear a word? Although you can find estimates (the one I use is that the learner needs to hear the word six times in the initial lesson and thirty more times in the ensuing month), there are obviously no hard-and-fast rules. It depends on whether the learner already knows parts of the word, especially the root. It depends also on how interested the learner is in the word, and how interesting or striking the context is. A word that is learned in the context of a story that evokes emotion has a better chance than one that is marched among many on a list of unrelated, decontextualized words.

Providing Quality Exposure to Words

Quality exposure to newly learned words is one of the most important things that an ordinary day in school can offer. The best exposure—the kind that results in the most durable learning—is helpful in context, well timed, multisensory, and question-based. Here are some ways to achieve these four features of quality exposure to words:

1. **Translate**: By "translate," we mean to layer your sentences so as to provide a built-in definition or example of words that you

think students might not fully know. Such built-in translation forms comprehensible input. Cynthia is a five-year-old who knows the meaning of the word *inappropriate* because her mother would talk to her like this: "Stop playing with your food. It's not nice. It's inappropriate. Don't turn your head and stare at that woman. It's impolite. It's inappropriate." Self-translation becomes a habit.

Another form of translation is rewording what children say to you. They speak to you in Tier I language, that is, the common words of informal conversation. You feed their language back to them with a dash of Tier II, that is, the more formal words of school, business, religion, and government. A child says, "I lost my book." You respond, "You misplaced it. Let's retrace your steps. When was the last time you had it in your hands?"

2. **Pre-visit, visit, revisit**: Applying the principle of spaced retrieval, you can casually introduce targeted words weeks before you intend to spend quality time with them, planting the words in the mind's peripheral vision. We'll call that a "pre-visit," which is a form of implicit instruction. In your writing mini-lessons, you might teach students that "one way writers draw their readers into the worlds of their stories is to write about a setting that creates a very specific climate for the reader." In this way, not only are you attending to the pre-visit, visit, revisit model of vocabulary instruction, you are also setting children up to learn a word that can be used in many different grade-level contexts and forms. After the word has been explicitly taught, make it a part of your classroom world. This is obvious, but when we isolate our vocabulary instruction, moving from one arbitrary list in a workbook to another, we may consider the necessity for continuous exposure unnecessary after the quiz has been taken, graded, and shelved. Don't shelve those valuable new words!

3. **Provide multisensory input**: We will say more about multisensory processing in Chapters 3 and 4. For now, just keep in mind that learning is strongly reinforced when it comes through the senses and is animated through facial expressions, hand gestures, and gross motor activity. Students who hear the words, say the words, quickly draw the words, find pictures that illustrate the words, act out the words, write the words, read the words, and even feel the words through tactile experiences decrease the likelihood of forgetting. A good, properly used word

wall functions like a billboard, and companies pay for billboards for a reason.

The Noticing Hypothesis

A metacognitive strategy that capitalizes on exposure is, simply enough, noticing words. We've all had the experience of hearing a new word or phrase, and then, oddly enough, we suddenly run into that word again and again. How did I get through life not knowing this word? Now I hear it all the time! One explanation could be that we heard the word in the first place because it happens to be buzzing around, for some reason. But another reason is that our awareness of a word that was there all the time is now in the foreground of our consciousness as a result of our just having learned it. That is to say, once you are aware of the existence of a word, you start paying attention to it, as if it had never crossed your path before, even though it probably did. In fact, there's a name for this phenomenon. It's called the "Noticing Hypothesis" as defined by Richard Schmidt (1990, 2001).

The Noticing Hypothesis rests on the fact that lots and lots of stimuli bombard us. We cannot pay attention to all of it, thus lots of stimuli get ignored. The job of teachers (insert prayer of choice here) is to focus our students' attention, in this case, on words that they don't yet know well. The more they notice such words, the sooner those words can get on to their rightful business of being . . . well, unnoticed (just part of the internal word inventory). Noticing the presence and forms of targeted words facilitates durable learning because noticing counts as a moment of exposure.

We can put the Noticing Hypothesis into service by asking students to notice the use of a handful of words on the Academic Word List (AWL) in their science, social studies, or math textbooks. (You will find them there in greater profusion than you would in a fictional story.) The words drawn from literature that you choose for explicit instruction should appear multiple times in the story for the Noticing Hypothesis to work well.

Your word walls may or may not include definitions, contexts, or illustrations. The most important feature of a word wall is that it is clear to the eye. Avoid clutter. If you want to include definitions, contexts, or illustrations, have enough white space to allow for easy reading from any distance within the classroom.

It's also important for students to put their new words in their hands as they write. Students across all grades can have personal word walls in their writing folders. These are, basically, lists of words that are high frequency for a particular child. If Joanna consistently writes about her life as a soccer player, her personal word wall might have words like, "goalkeeper," "cleats," and "penalty." Offer word banks as a prewriting scaffold and again as a revision scaffold. When students are writing about literature, have them pull "special" words right out of the text, words that they can incorporate into their writing pieces. These words can be added onto their personal word walls, too.

Ask Easy Questions

Start with yes-no and this-or-that questions, and have students use the targeted word in their answers, even though it will sound redundant. This is a way to provide meaningful repetition.

Let's say you are working with the picture book *Amos & Boris* by William Steig (1971). This lovely book has a grade level equivalent of 3.7 (Scholastic. com), but because it is a picture book, it is appropriate for K–2 as a read-aloud. It weaves sophisticated vocabulary with a simple, attractively illustrated story, making it comprehensible. It's a story about a mouse (Amos) and a whale (Boris). Here's the text on page 5, describing the boat that Amos just built for the voyage that proceeds in the story:

> The Rodent, for that was the boat's name, proved to be very well made and very well suited to the sea. And Amos, after one miserable day of seasickness, proved to be a natural sailor, very well suited to the ship.
>
> He was enjoying the trip immensely. It was beautiful weather. Day and night he moved up and down, up and down, on waves as big as mountains, and he was full of wonder, full of enterprise, and full of love for life.

I'm reading this book to first graders. The gist is easy for them to get, but, as you can see, many of the words are unfamiliar or used in unfamiliar ways. Our targeted word is *immensely*.

Yes–no and this-or-that statements

Put your hand up if you think the word *immensely* means that Amos was enjoying the trip a lot or a little.

Put your hand up if you think the beautiful weather was part of the reason why Amos was enjoying the trip immensely.

> Put your hand up if you think immensely means big or small.
> Put your hand up if you think Amos is an immense creature.
> We haven't met Boris yet, but Boris is a whale. Put your hand up if you think Boris is immense.

Then there's the way the word *proved* is used. Some first graders may know that proving something has to do with guaranteeing that it is true. Questions to broaden their understanding of this word in context might be these:

> The boat proved to be very well made, and Amos proved to be a natural sailor. Do you think the trip proved to be enjoyable? Do you think Amos proved to be excited about this trip? Do you think it proved to be miserable weather?

We could do the same with the phrase *well suited to*. Both *proved to be* and *well suited to* may fly under our radar as we consider unknown vocabulary in text, but it's important that we consider not just words alone, but words that may be used in unfamiliar ways.

The text says that Amos is full of enterprise. I would never expect first graders to know that word, but the context is helpful enough for them to be able to think through questions like whether "being full of enterprise" is good or bad, what are synonyms and antonyms for "enterprise," and so on. You can sprinkle these questions into students' turn-and-talk and/or stop-and-jot opportunities. This might sound something like this:

> Turn and tell your partner whether you think "being full of enterprise" is a good or bad thing. How do you know? Use what you know from the story to help you.
>
> Stop and jot on your sticky note: What is another word that means the same thing as "enterprise"?

I hope you noticed that I changed the form of the words as I asked the questions. Part of the repeated exposure principle is that words need to be presented in various forms as well as contexts.

Experts in language acquisition agree that the critical factor in word-learning is repeated, substantive exposure, the kind of exposure that, collectively, gradually employs a word in its full range of meaning and grammatical forms. In the next chapter, we will explain how examples that represent a word are an important element of instruction and can even be more instructive than definitions.

"Word of the Day"

Many teachers and schools attempt to teach vocabulary in the form of a "word of the day." This can be effective, but it usually is not. Here are some of the problems I've seen with "word of the day":

1. The "word of the day" comes from nowhere.
2. The "word of the day" disappears at the end of the day.
3. Little information is given about the "word of the day."
4. The "word of the day" is thought to suffice as vocabulary instruction.

"Word of the day" practices can be effective if a well-chosen word is presented in a meaningful way and then kept alive beyond its special day. To make "word of the day" more sticky, try several of these enhancements:

1. Selection: Rather than just marching through a list, pick your "word of the day" mindfully. There has to be something going on in the world outside your school's walls that sparks an idea for a word. Be inspired by your local newspaper. That way, your word has an automatic context, and your "word of the day" program serves the double purpose of providing background knowledge about the world.
2. Post your "word of the day" on your word wall *and use it in the days to come.* Your "word of the day" should be useful enough to enhance your vocabulary, and that of your students, easily (or perhaps your word is too obscure). If you are doing this right, you will find that you are using the word in various morphological forms and contexts.
3. If a word is worth "word of the day" status, then it is also worth ten minutes of close-up investigation. Create a semantic map (a visual representation that includes various dimensions of a word: synonyms and near-synonyms; antonyms and near-antonyms; morphological forms; prefixes, roots, and suffixes, if applicable; interesting etymology, if applicable; quick visual representation; a quotation, if possible. Keep your semantic map posted, and have students copy it into their notebooks at

some point during the day. (They don't all have to do that at the same time in reading–writing workshop.)

4. Realize that "word of the day" is one component of vocabulary instruction, which should be infused throughout the day as both implicit and explicit instruction.

Key Points

1. Your classroom may be the only place where children are exposed to academic vocabulary. This is especially true for children who live in poverty and those who are English-language learners. You need to develop the habit of speaking to children using elevated vocabulary, but support words that children may not know with helpful, revealing contexts. We call such contexts comprehensible input.

2. Because words are absorbed over time, we need to keep words in play for many days, and then not forget about them as the school year progresses. Words that are crammed for a quiz but then faded from the eyes and ears will probably be forgotten. We call the practice of revisiting previously taught words *spaced retrieval* or *distributed practice*.

3. Students need guided opportunities to use their new words. We can cue targeted words as word banks during the prewriting and revision stages of the writing process.

4. We need to coax students' awareness of the words we've taught as they listen and read. Awareness alone constitutes a form of meaningful exposure. Experts in language acquisition call this the Noticing Hypothesis.

5. To practice and reinforce new words, we can ask a series of easy questions that require the use of the targeted word, both receptively (teacher talk) and productively (student talk). We should engage the whole group in giving answers to our questions ("Put your hand up if you think . . .") rather than calling on individual students while others sit by.

Repeated exposure with comprehensible input (helpful context) alone will grow vocabulary. But not enough. Students need to learn information about word components. This information allows them to use strategies for figuring out new words, especially multisyllabic ones. In the next chapter, we'll explain the what, why, and how of teaching words explicitly and thoroughly through **exploration**.

Bibliography

Coxhead, Averil. (2006). *Essentials of Teaching Academic Vocabulary.* Boston, MA: Houghton Mifflin. 20.

Dabrowska, Ewa. (2015). *Handbook of Cognitive Linguistics.* Berlin/Boston: Walter de Gruyter GmbH. 58.

Joe, Angela. (April 2010). The Quality and Frequency of Encounters With Vocabulary in an English for Academic Purposes Programme. *Reading in a Foreign Language*, 22(1), 117–138.

Pappano, Laura. (May/June, 2008). Small Kids, Big Words. *Harvard Education Letter*, 24(3), 1.

Robertson, Dana, Evelyn Ford-Connors and Jeanne R. Paratore. (July, 2014). Coaching Teachers' Talk During Vocabulary and Comprehension Instruction. *Language Arts*, 91(6), 416–427.

Rylant, Cynthia. (1997). *Poppleton.* New York: Scholastic. 10.

Schmidt, R. (1990). The Role of Consiousness in Second Language Learning. *Applied Linguistics*, 11, 129–158.

Schmidt, R. (2001). Attention. In P. Robinson (Ed.), *Cognition and second language instruction* (pp. 3–32). Cambridge: Cambridge University Press.

Schmidt, Richard. (2010). *Attention, Awareness, and Individual Differences in Language Learning.* Manoa, HI: The University of Hawaii. 1.

Stahl, Steven A. (Spring, 2003). How Words Are Learned Incrementally Over Multiple Exposures. *AFT*, 18.

Steig, Willliam. (1971). *Amos & Boris.* New York: Farrar, Straus and Giroux.

2

Exploration

"A word is not a crystal, transparent and unchanged; it is the skin of a living thought and may vary greatly in color and content according to the circumstance and time in which it is used."

Oliver Wendell Holmes

A major weakness in vocabulary instruction is that we favor quantity of words over quality of instruction on *each* word. Students often only memorize brief definitions, easily forgettable. But we have only so much time for direct vocabulary instruction in a busy workshop, and we know that the number of words students need to know cannot possibly be addressed by thorough instruction on each one. We acknowledge the limits of instructional time. So word selection is important. In teaching a rich word deeply—by extensive exploration, as is about to be demonstrated—you can actually teach multiple words and word-learning strategies simultaneously in the mini-lesson. Well-chosen words, thoroughly explored, magnetize other words. Applying this principle, you will end up giving your students a greater yield of words than you would with the traditional practice, where students do little more than memorize brief definitions, especially when given a list of unrelated words.

This chapter will explain in detail how you can teach words deeply by thoughtfully selecting and organizing words for explicit instruction, and then teaching them with awareness of principles of both language acquisition and sound pedagogy. Reliable, consistent vocabulary growth does depend on a multifaceted approach. I'll say again that exposure and context alone will not grow students' vocabulary as much as is necessary. We need some explicit instruction, and we need to use our time for it wisely. In his book *Building Background Knowledge for Academic Achievement* (2004), Robert Marzano says, "Direct vocabulary instruction has an impressive track record of improving students' background knowledge and the comprehension of academic content" (69). Explicit vocabulary instruction *must* be included, whether we think it "fits in" to reading–writing workshop or not. To make the best use of limited time, let's think about word selection, organization of targeted words, effective ways of introducing words, considerations about words that represent abstract concepts, using visuals, etymology dimensions of word knowledge, and then five models for explicit instruction.

Strategy 1: Select Useful and Productive Words

Wise selection of words is crucial. Here are some suggestions for selecting words relating to literature. To have a sampling of words to work with, we're using *Frog and Toad Together* (Arnold Lobel, 1971), which is appropriate for a read-aloud to kindergarten or grade 1. Here are the words in that book that might be candidates for explicit instruction: *wailed, swamp, gasped, will power, leaping, avalanche, trembling, presenting, peeped, lonely, frightened.* Here are some words from the first three pages of *Castle Diary: The Journal of Tobias Burgess* (Richard Platt, 1999, illustrated by Chris Riddell), which we'll say is at the fourth-grade level: *parish, dwell, page, squire, mayhap, bid, 'tis, scarce, tries, vex, knight, manor house, courtyard, pallets.* You'll notice that many of these words are used in unfamiliar ways in the context of a description of medieval castle life; others are archaic. And, for the middle schoolers, we'll pull some words from *Bud, Not Buddy* (Christopher Paul Curtis, 1999): *commence, glum, twine, provoke, urchin, vermin, embouchure, prodigy, hue.* You see from these samplings that not all words that are unknown to students are equally important to know, and the extent to which we can learn about them also varies. Some words simply deserve more attention than others.

1. **Select a useful word.** Don't be guilty of what I call the Novelty Word Syndrome: I was working as a consultant in a very low-performing district, where almost all the children lived in urban poverty. While waiting for my group of teachers to arrive for their session with me, I observed a group of fifth graders studying a vocabulary list for a social studies test. They had a list of words that had been drawn up

(from the publisher, not the teacher) from the chapter "Regions of Our Country." The children were working on a matching column. I noticed that one of their words was *megalopolis*. Although they were able to match *megalopolis* with its definition, *interrelated cluster of nearby cities*, I wondered if their vocabulary/social studies time could not be better spent. After all, the word *megalopolis* has a frequency of 41,337 (vocabulary.com/dictionary). That means, you would theoretically have to read 41,337 words before encountering the word *megalopolis* one time. Not a big yield. Compare that to the word *metropolis*, which has a frequency of 393, making it about as frequent—in general text—as the words *urban* (365) and *rural* (348). So, just how useful is the word *megalopolis* to a fifth grader? Does that fifth grader know the far more useful and relevant word *metropolis*? or *metropolitan*? All other things being equal, it is hard to justify selecting highly infrequent words for instruction to students whose academic success depends on the *frequent* words that they don't know yet. I call this the Novelty Word Syndrome, and I've seen it with words like *succotash, archipelago, daimyo* (in what context would the word *succotash*, with a frequency of 49,454, not indicate that succotash is some kind of food? Should this word be a priority?) With novelty words like this, you can just touch upon them briefly if students are curious about them, or if their meaning is necessary for understanding a particular passage.

Online Tools

Online tools for finding out the frequency of particular words are invaluable. The one in Vocabulary.com (www.vocabulary.com/dictionary) is my favorite. This resource will give you a student-friendly definition on the left side and, on the right side, will give you all of the morphological forms (prefixes and suffixes) listed as "Word Family." If you hover your cursor over any of the words listed there, the frequency number will pop up, telling you how many pages you can expect to read before encountering that word once. The frequency ranking will help you enormously in deciding which words are worth an investment of your instructional time.

2. **Select a word that you think some children already know something about.** The idea of doing this is to help children develop and trust

their intuition about words by looking for possible leads within words whose parts they recognize. This includes Spanish cognates (and cognates in other Latin-based languages).

3. **Select "high-yield" words.** Try to leverage knowledge of one word into knowledge of several related words. We will say more later in this chapter about what it means to teach words in clusters. Remember that a single bit of isolated information will probably be forgotten, but a word (or fact) that is part of a meaning-based bundle has a far greater chance of survival in the busy brain. When it comes to vocabulary, we're catching fish in the deep blue sea, not the backyard swimming pool. We're fishing for the big tuna, but other fish get caught in the net, and we don't toss them back.

4. **Select words that illustrate a spelling pattern.** Many words are right there in children's oral vocabularies, but the children don't recognize them in writing because of silent letters or unfamiliar letter combinations. For example, a young reader may not recognize the word *frightened* in writing. Teaching that word gives us the opportunities to connect it, spelling-wise, to the words *light, lighten, lightest, lightning, bright, brighten, brighter, brightest.*

Strategy 2: Organize Your Word List

Consider these four word lists, each drawn from *Julie of the Wolves* (1972) by Jean Craighead George:

> List A (words selected because they appear in the novel): *predicament, regal, discern, lure, gesture, hostile, instill, frigid, instinct, evoke*
>
> List B (words selected because they pertain to a single concept relevant to this novel): *predicament, dilemma, plight, quandary, option, alternative, decisive, indecisive, tentative, perplex*
>
> List C (words selected because they cluster around either of two Latin roots, and because most of them are relevant to this novel): *survive, revive, vivid, vivacious, vital, vitality, vitamin, option, optional, opt, adopt*
>
> List D (words selected because they name different animals that are mentioned in this novel): *jaegers, sandpipers, puffins, plover, caribou, cod, halibut, tern, wolverine, snowshoe hare, weasel, lemming, eider duck, ptarmigan*
>
> List E (words selected because they appear at least once in the novel and are specific, technical terms relevant to life in the Arctic regions, which is the setting of the novel): *quonset, parka, subzero, tundra, mainland, frostbite, gussak, hide, lichen, ulo*

> List F (words selected along with the phrases in which they appear in the novel because this phraseology is typical for these words): *holding him in abeyance, brandishing her weapon, she listened intently, flailing her hands and feet*

Lists B–F are far more likely to result in durable learning than List A, which is a random collection of words related *only* by the fact that they happen to appear in a single book. Although a list like this is often justified as being words "taken from the literature," it ends up being only slightly better than any other list of arbitrary words. In contrast, the words in Lists B–E, because of their organization around a single theme, allow for better instruction. In List B, words pertaining to a single concept, in this case, decision-making, include nouns, adjectives, and one verb. A student could use several of these words to describe a moment either in *Julie of the Wolves* or in her own life.

The words in List C derive from common Latin roots *vivre* (to live) and *optare* (to choose, to wish). This is an opportunity to explain that the words *vital, vitality*, and even *vitamin* derive from the *vivre* family, even though their spellings have evolved from the *viv-* to the *vit-*. We include *vitamin* on the list, which we assume to be familiar to students, only to anchor them to their existing knowledge about this word root. As for *optare*, this is a root that lives in close proximity to three other Latin sound-alikes: *optimus*, meaning best (*optimum, optimal*) and *optics*, meaning *sight* (*optical, optician, Cyclops*) and *operari*, meaning *done by labor* (*operate, opus, opera*).

List D is just a catalog of items, in this case, animals that are mentioned in the novel. Students may know what many of these animals look like, and it isn't necessary for them to know much more than that, for the purposes of understanding this story and expanding their background knowledge. We wouldn't do much more than have them locate pictures of these animals and perhaps arrange them by categories (birds, fish, mammals). Students could, perhaps, write brief reports about one of these creatures, or create a display for the class.

List E has the technical, domain-specific (a.k.a. Tier III) terms that are relevant to *Julie of the Wolves*. All of these words appear multiple times and are necessary for comprehension, although several of them are extremely specific and may never be encountered outside of the Arctic Circle. Pictures of these are easy to find. You might show a picture of a parka, for example, alongside a picture of a trench coat and a ski jacket, and have students do some "concept attainment" to determine what makes a parka a parka.

List F is a little different. It is based on the linguistic concept called *collocation*. Some words almost always come in predictable phrases. When a student learns these words singly, detached from their phrases, that is insufficient. Have you ever heard or used the word *abeyance* without preceding it with the word *hold/holding/held in*? If I tell you that someone is *brandishing* something, don't you expect it to be some kind of weapon, or something being used as a weapon? If someone is doing something *intently*, aren't they usually listening or looking? When was the last time you heard of anyone *flailing* anything but their arms? Possible, but unlikely. As you glean vocabulary words from literature, be on the lookout for collocations. They allow learners to properly use a new word in its favorite context, which makes the word ready to go.

How many of your mini-lessons can center on vocabulary? Not all of them, for sure. Your mini-lesson schedule needs to include grammar, metacognitive strategies, author's craft, story structure, and, sometimes, the author's background and historical/geographical information. Let's say you can clear the decks for one or two mini-lessons devoted to vocabulary each week. (Aim for one mini-lesson one week, two the next.) With such a limited amount of time, you need to select words that open doors to other words *and* word-learning strategies.

The best words to choose for exploration are those that, for one reason or another, are rich in secondary benefits, that is, other words that are conveniently gleaned in the course of exploring the target word, the way smaller fish are inadvertently snagged in the tuna fisherman's net. So when selecting words to bring front and center for explicit instruction, consider the spin-off opportunities available for instruction.

The idea is to spin a web around a word so that the students are learning clusters, rather than single words. (Isolated facts tend to "fall to the bottom" of the brain and are hard to retrieve.) Some of the words that surround our target word should be words we think students already know; some should be words we think they know partially; and then a few others can be words that are probably new. The reason for that combination is so that students will have familiar information on which to build, while at the same time deepening knowledge of partially known words, and introducing new ones *in the context* of known information.

The value of exploration as a means of explicit teaching of a word is that we are spending quality time setting up a web of associations. The quality time involves meaningful repetition in the course of explaining relationships among words. The associations allow the word to lock into multiple mental "places." Words are explorable in different ways, depending on their structure, meaning, and use. As we've said, to teach a word thoroughly is to exceed brief definitions. Brief definitions are a quick visit, and they have their use when we need to move ahead in the here and now, as in a read-aloud. We expect spotty results from giving brief definitions, and that's fine:

we don't have the time to teach more than eight to ten words a week explicitly and thoroughly, so quick definitions have a place.

Strategy 3: Make Connections When Introducing New Words

Learning requires thinking. When we say at the outset, "The word X means Y," we have not given students processing time to think. While we've acknowledged that there are many times when we have to just give a quick definition and move on, if you are doing explicit instruction on a well-chosen target word, even during a mini-lesson, consider giving students a little time to prepare their minds to receive a new word that names a concept that they already know. They may know the concept by another name, or the concept may be floating namelessly in their brains. For example, suppose you were teaching about pioneer life to second graders. You want them to know the names of different phases of a journey, words that describe survival skills, and words for different kinds of land. You want them to know the word *prairie*. You could show them a picture of a prairie and ask them what they notice about it. With their input, you compile a list of features. Some of these will be relevant and essential to the concept. Others, such as "has flowers," are features, but not distinguishing features, of a prairie. When the list has five or six items, you remove the nonessential ones, and what you have left is a list of defining features of a prairie. "And there's a name for this kind of land. We call it a prairie." *The new word names a known concept.*

"And there's a name for what we've been talking about. We call it _____." This is the golden moment in explicit vocabulary instruction. From here, we can explore a word whose concept is known. There's a name for this kind of concept-to-word teaching. We call it *integration.* You are getting students to integrate a new term into their existing understanding of the world.

Introducing a word through the technique of integration is not always easy, probably not always possible. But because it is powerful, you should do this whenever you can. Anytime a word can be clearly and unambiguously connected to a visual, you should show the visual and lead a conversation about its salient features *before* introducing the target word.

Inductive Reasoning through Pictures

A memorable way to introduce words is through visuals that invite thinking about attributes. Here is the procedure:

Target word: *aerie* (a nest that is built high in a tree or in a high window)

First, show two pictures that each depict an aerie. Be careful to select pictures in which the aerie (high nest) is the only commonality. There may be an eagle in one picture, but not in both, lest the student draw an unintended conclusion.

Then, show three new pictures, only one of which depicts an aerie. One of the non-aerie pictures can show a nest on the ground, and the other can show a flying eagle. It should be fairly easy to conclude which of the pictures depicts an aerie.

At this point, it should be possible to write a definition, or at least to identify the distinguishing characteristics of an aerie.

This procedure can be used to introduce any word that can be represented by a picture.

All words are related to other words. The relationships that come easiest to mind are synonyms (or near-synonyms), antonyms (near-antonyms), and same-topic relationships. In considering a word like *habitat*, we can use it as a general term for which there are examples that we could also learn at the same time. Our students already know that animals live in broadly named habitats such as oceans, forests, cities. Now they can strengthen their understanding of the word *habitat* by being more specific: *deciduous forest, coniferous forest, rain forest*; *treeless habitats* break down into *grasslands* and *tundra*. The more organized a word grouping is, the more meaning it will have and the more retrievable it will be.

Now, think of how we can place *habitat* as an item within a larger category: Facts about Living Things. When we learn about living things, we learn about their habitats. We also learn about their structures, their means of defense, their diets, their social habits, how they reproduce, and so on. We're building a constellation of words around a single targeted word, *habitat*.

Once you think in terms of the relationships among words, you can make informed decisions about how to organize them visually. Unfortunately, what often happens is that students are given a vertical list of words about a topic, where the visual impact of the list is not helpful in understanding the relationship among words. This is a missed opportunity.

Strategy 4: Be Mindful of the Challenges of Abstract Words

Words for abstract concepts are trickier. The further up in grade levels we go, the more the vocabulary represents abstract concepts and assumes that the student can toggle from concrete to abstract and back again. Most of the words on the Coxhead Academic Word List (AWL) represent abstract concepts. It can be hard or impossible to convert words for abstract concept into pictures. Words name abstract concepts, but the concepts themselves are not learned just because we know the definition of a word. Knowing the word for an abstract concept is like having an icon on your computer screen: a given icon is a mere representation, not the thing itself. A word for an abstract concept is known truly when the learner can apply the concept to a new embodiment of it, or when she can transfer.

In 1940, the linguist and philosopher S. I. Hayakawa wrote *Language in Thought and Action* (with Alan Hayakawa) to explain how the words we use succeed or fail in capturing, and even in forming, thought. Hayakawa discusses how important it is to place words along a continuum of concreteness and abstractness. Using the term *ladder of abstraction*, Hayakawa illustrates how humans think, beginning with basic and accessible (concrete and specific) and moving up the ladder of abstraction to more general, intangible concepts. This is a powerful notion, and we can use it to help students build the kind of vocabulary that we use in school (and business).

Understanding where words fit on the ladder of abstraction helps us explore and expand it. Let's work with a simplified form of Hayakawa's ladder of abstraction, using just three levels (Hayakawa's model uses up to eight levels).

The following examples will help you understand the ladder of abstraction. Note that the ladder is a flexible model. More than one response is possible. But if you bring this model into your word explorations, you will be helping students become sharper thinkers about words and the world. We create ladders of abstractions for two reasons: (1) to develop the rudimentary understanding about what abstractions are, as higher-level thinking depends on using abstractions, and (2) to afford opportunities for building different kinds of vocabulary about a concept, including both concrete examples and the abstract concepts that corral them into a larger category.

Example 1:

> Level 1: bicycle (most specific)
> Level 2: vehicles (establishing a group)
> Level 3: transportation (abstract noun)

Example 2:

> Level 1: aerie
> Level 2: home
> Level 3: shelter

Example 3:

> Level 1: sister
> Level 2: family
> Level 3: relationships

Example 4:

> Level 1: tree
> Level 2: wood
> Level 3: building materials

Example 5:

> Level 1: birthday card
> Level 2: birthday
> Level 3: celebration

Strategy 5: Include Etymology: The Power Source for Understanding Academic Words

Etymology is fascinating. There's something delightful about discovering connections, making order out of chaos. Etymology gives students tools to investigate words. Broadly speaking, there are two kinds of etymology:

1. Stories about single words: words that entered the language, one at a time, through interesting histories.
2. Latin and Greek roots: words that entered the language as offshoots from Latin and Greek roots.

Many examples of "interesting history" words come to us by way of Greek mythology. Out of these stories and characters come words like *atlas, tantalize, labyrinth, hypnotize, nemesis, mentor, chronological,* and *typhoon* (from Typhon, father of monsters). Words that used to be the names of people (or gods) are called eponyms. Many eponyms are named after actual people who once lived and made something about themselves so famous that their name entered the language: *boycott, diesel, algorithm, silhouette,* and *maverick.* Often these words have a unique sound that makes them hard to remember. But stories are memorable.

There are words whose connotations have changed over time, but we have fossils of their former meanings. For example, if you were referring to a person who had achieved only the lowest rank at the university level, would you use the word *bachelor*? That is probably not what the word *bachelor* means to you. Yet, we still have the phrase *bachelor's degree*, where the word retains its long-ago meaning. Is a *gymnasium* a place in which to play games naked? For the Greeks, who made up this word, it was. Shakespeare used the word *cousin* to refer to uncles and nephews. We apply a more narrow meaning. And who today could use the word *awesome* only to refer something that is, well, awe-inspiring. That's a word that has become so loose in meaning, your waiter says it when all you did was order your meal.

Latin Word Roots: One Will Get You Ten

As many as 60% of the words in English are derived from Latin and Greek. While the common prefixes and suffixes are usually taught, sets of useful Latin roots are usually not. And they should be. If elementary schools had a scope and sequence for teaching as few as twenty Latin roots, students would learn more than hundreds of useful words. They would also learn how to look at words analytically. They would be less intimidated by multisyllabic words because they would have tools.

As it happens, words with Latin and Greek roots tend to be those words that we use to talk about knowledge and abstract ideas. Our Tier II and III words are loaded up with Latin and Greek components. That is not a chance happening. English is an amalgamated language whose basic, and oldest, words come from German (the Anglo-Saxon tribal hordes that took hold of the land early centuries of the first millennium). That Germanic language became mixed with Norse when the Vikings came to town in the eighth century. The change in management that took place after 1066 brought in a whole new layer of Latin (via French). The significance of this, to this day, is that the English language is bi-leveled, with the so-called simple, Germanic-Norse words that we're calling Tier I and the "fancier," more abstract Latinate words that we're calling Tier II. As a result of new learnings and even more abstract notions of the Renaissance, another layer, Greek, forms many of the words that we consider Tier III.

You get a tenfold return on your investment for teaching each of the Latin roots in Appendix B: Remember that the best vocabulary lists have words that are related to each other. These words are all related by the common ancestry of a shared meaning. Also, the best vocabulary lists offer a combination of familiar words, partially known words, and new words.

Strategy 6: Teach the Dimensions of Word Knowledge

Most words do not have single, finite meanings. Dictionaries account for this. You can read through all of the dictionary definitions for a word, but that is not how the various shades of meanings for words are learned. Vocabulary knowledge may be considered in two ways: the number of words that a person knows is one way; the depth to which she knows those words and the flexibility in which she can use them is another. Rich, flexible knowledge of a word is accrued incrementally, primarily through repeated exposure in a variety of contexts and forms, but through skillful explicit instruction as well.

To know a word is to know its surface characteristics: its pronunciation and (reasonable representation of) its spelling. A surface characteristic of a word includes its morphological forms: If a noun, does it pluralize? If so, does it pluralize by adding *-s*, *-es*, or an irregular form? If its default form is something other than a noun, what noun-making suffixes (*-tion/-sion*, *-ence/-ance*, *-ity*, *-itude*, *-ism*, *-hood*, etc.) can it accept? If it can be used as a verb, it will follow the predictable path of verb formations, but what do its past and perfect forms look like? Are they regular or irregular? (Almost all Tier II and Tier III verbs are regular.) If its default form is not a verb, what verb-making suffixes (*-ize*, *-ate*, *-ify*, etc.) can it accept? Do we change the spelling of the stem form to add *-ing*? If its default form is not an adjective, what adjective-making suffixes (*-y*, *-ious*, *-able*, *-ible*, etc.) can it accept? Can it morph into an adverb by adding the suffix *-ly*? Morphological explorations can be recorded on a four-column chart (noun, verb, adjective, adverb). These charts are actually fun to create, as they lead to nonexistent word forms that children (and adults) find amusing, for some reason rooted in the human tendency to find nonsense words giggle-worthy. If you do morphological charts with your students, it's a good idea to have a dictionary-checker, as knowing whether a "word is a real word" when you add an ending to it gets a little murky. Prefixes are also part of morphology, although they change the meaning, usually into the opposite, while the suffixes change the grammatical applicability.

To know a word is to know its attitude, its track record, its tendencies. Is it a formal, technical word? A conversational, everyday word? A slang word? A polite way of saying something unpleasant (euphemism)? Does it evoke a negative, insulting feeling (dysphemism, e.g., *"rape the natural world" instead of "pollute the planet"*)? To what category does it belong? Where does it fit in an array of other members of that category? How frequent is it in the language? Is it a word that educated people are expected to know? (You can find the frequency of a word—that is, how many pages would it probably take to find one instance of a given word?—by going to Vocabulary.com's dictionary. Hover your cursor over the word family entries on the right, and the frequency will pop up. The words *predicament* and *dilemma* are in the same ballpark of frequency [1,803 and 1,021, respectively], while the word *quandary* is much rarer, with a frequency of 6,933. But the word *plight* has a relatively high frequency: 746. All other things equal, a word's frequency is the most reliable predictor of how "hard" we think a word is, but "hard" words are really just infrequent words, and the way to turn infrequent words into frequent words is to use them—frequently. This, we do in the course of exploration.)

And to know a word is to know its *collocational properties*, a fancy way of saying, "Word A and Words B and C are often seen together." There may not be a reason for these go-togethers. Their proximity is probably just a tradition that has developed in the way people talk. For example, we often say *round of applause* (not *bunch of applause* or *round of approval*), *burst into tears* (not *burst into weeping* or *suddened into tears*), *commit crime* (not *commit marriage* or *got crimed*). Collocations, closely related to figures of speech or clichés, are "just the way." Not knowing a word's collocation, if it has one, is like serving red wine with fish. There's no law against it, but you look like you don't know the code.

Bridges to Spelling

If we neglect to make spelling part of vocabulary instruction, we may be diminishing the chances that students will use their newly learned words. Like adults, students tend to avoid writing words that they don't know how to spell. Vocabulary and spelling instruction can be mutually supportive. The English language is not as unpredictable and unreliable as you might think. Many times, if we take the trouble to learn the inside story of spelling, we solidify our understanding of related words, and vice versa.

Because exposure refers to the eyes as well as the ears, repeated exposure to the written word has implications for spelling. As any solver of crossword puzzles, word searches, anagrams, or cryptograms knows, certain letter combinations are predictable, others are rare, and others are never seen in the English language.

Many people just roll their eyes and dismiss English spelling patterns as "crazy." The problem with doing this is that "crazy things"—things without a method to their madness—are impossible to learn through systematic thinking or reasoning. Isolated bits of information can only be memorized, and that's a lot of mental labor, which is not only time-consuming but insufficient. Memorization of words, one at a time, would be unnecessary if we could acknowledge existing patterns and relationships among words and word parts. Seeing spelling patterns helps us do this.

We need to find what the linguists call *systematicity* in English spelling wherever we can, because learning the patterns will make spelling easier to learn and remember. But first, I'd like to use a little history and etymology to scare away some of the goblins of English spelling.

The English language is layered in a way that recapitulates its history. Its first known phase is called the Anglo-Saxon period (beginning in the first century AD), where English was a kind of Germanic blend, highly influenced by Norse, Flemish, and Danish languages. Our most basic and concrete words have been in the language since this time. Words with a -*gh* and -*ght* combination were pronounced with a guttural sound, not silent as they are in our lifetimes. What we know as the silent *e* was, in those days, a pronounced syllable. And the sounds of English changed in other ways over the centuries. Knowing this may or may not make a child a better speller, but it does provide an answer to the questions about why English spelling is not more phonetically true. Think of people from various villages converging on a developing city—London, in fact. The villagers contribute their own branded styles of speech, which all eventually get mixed together in use, but retain their distinctive village characteristics as to how they appear when encoded (spelling). To make matters more complex, the Anglo-Saxon alphabet had only twenty-seven letters (graphemes) but the language needed to represent forty sounds (phonemes). With letters having to do double duty, spelling becomes less phonetic than it is in some other languages, such as Spanish.

The Anglo-Saxon tongue became layered with Latinate words, mostly relating to the Church, during the four centuries (beginning with the arrival of St. Augustine in 597) when the land that we know as England became part of the Roman Empire. But that change in the language was relatively small, compared to the estimated 10,000 French words that dropped into English during the Norman occupation (launched by William the Conqueror in 1066). We and our students may not be aware of it, but that period of English history when the French held sway affects us daily, because of where those French words landed. They landed right in the precincts of power: law, art, literature, cuisine, and social manners.

The good news for spellers is that French is derived from Latin, and Latin-based words tend to be phonetic and obedient to rules about adding prefixes and suffixes. (See the AWL in Appendix B.) The bad news for spellers is that many of those French words and expressions survive intact, that is, still spelled the French way.

But it wasn't until 1476, when William Caxton established the first printing press in Westminster, that English spelling began to be standardized. Most books of that time were printed only in Latin, with a few in French. In a bold move, Caxton decided to print books on his press in English. Perceiving that the influences of the French nobility were on the downswing, Caxton bet on English being on the rise in his foreseeable future. Then, he faced another judgment call: Which of the several accents of English should he encode? He settled on the dialect of London, and so it came about that one of many dialects became enshrined in the spelling of English. "The proof of Caxton's influence, for good or bad, is still seen today. He fixed written English before it had actually 'reached a consensus'" (McCrum, in K.C.L., n.d.).

Dictionaries: Verification and Exploration

Students need to learn what dictionaries offer, how they are arranged, that there are different kinds of dictionaries, and efficient ways to use them for given purposes. Think about how *you* use a dictionary. You probably use it to clarify the definition of a word that you have actually encountered. You probably use it as close to the time you encountered the word as possible, if not immediately. And when you read the definition, you probably were not very surprised, as you probably already had some idea about what the word meant in the context in which you encountered it. Perhaps you consulted a dictionary to settle a disagreement in a social or business setting about what a word meant. When *you* use a dictionary, you probably use it to *verify* your guess about a word that interests you.

When was the last time you expanded your vocabulary by being told to find and copy definitions for a list of alphabetized, decontextualized words organized by no particular principle? Do you think you would learn a word by copying out a definition if you didn't know the meaning of the words in that definition? How long do you think you would retain the dictionary definition of *that* word?

Dictionaries are invaluable tools for exploring words deeply. Rather than having students "fetch and retrieve" the first (or shortest) definition, students can have an activity that calls for spending quality time with the entire entry—pronunciation, shades of meaning, morphological forms, affixes, etymology, and, of course, spelling. But students need a purpose to extract and understand this information. That is where games, puzzles, and social activities come in (see Chapter 4).

Incidentally, you will find student-friendly, full-bodied, memorable, meaningful, and interesting definitions that include examples and connect the word to relatable experiences at Vocabulary.com.

Five Models for Explicit Instruction

Following is a summary of five models described in various places in this book for explicit instruction for your technical terminology and literary words, which are the kinds of words found in stories but not often in the conversations that your students hear in everyday speech.

What these models have in common is that they allow students sufficient processing time for learning and remembering the words. You don't have to use more than one model for a given word, but you can combine them for even more durable learning.

Model I: Inductive Reasoning through Visuals

1. Select a word that lends itself to a clear visual. The word will probably be a noun.
2. Find and show two pictures that clearly represent the word. Show the word next to the pictures. Ask students to turn and talk about the attributes in the pictures: *What is everything you notice?*
3. Find and show two non-examples. Ask the students to turn and talk about why this might be a non-example of the targeted word: *What differences do you see?*
4. Present a fifth image that may or may not be an example of the target word, and ask students to turn and talk to determine whether it "fits" or "does not fit" and explain why.
5. Have students hypothesize a definition. Then, give them the official definition and have them adjust.

Why it works: This procedure is powerful because (1) visuals are informative and memorable; (2) the turn-and-talks allow students to learn through speaking and listening; and (3) inductive reasoning provides quality time with the word. Through it, the students "earn their knowledge" of the word, rather than having it handed to them.

Model II: Concept First

"AND THERE'S A NAME FOR THIS. WE CALL IT _____."

I've said many times in this book, in many ways, that just stating a definition is not the same as teaching a word so that it will stay learned. Although there are times when, in the interest of efficiency and priorities at a given moment, it is advisable to just "define quickly and move on," when we decide to spend quality time explicitly teaching a word, there is power in getting the students to "feel the concept" first, and *then* give it a name. There's a name for this kind of teaching: We call it *concept first*. (What I just did is an example of it.)

Try doing the concept-first method so many times that when you say, "And there's a name for this," the students chime right in with "We call it . . ."

Sometimes, we find writers who present terminology organically in the concept-first way. Look at this article by Jane Sullivan, which was on the New York State Assessments Grade 3 English Language Arts exam in 2015:

> ### "The Aurora Borealis"
>
> It's winter in Alaska—midnight—nine degrees above zero. And yet, there are people—grown-ups, bundled against the cold; children are clothed in scarves, gloves, and fur-lined boots, outside, looking at the sky. Why? It is because the sky is putting on a show for them, a show we call the northern lights. Scientists call it the aurora borealis.

The author in this narrative about a scientific concept opens the piece with a description of a story world, inviting the reader in, before introducing the terminology, and she even introduces the more familiar term *northern lights* before presenting the scientific term *aurora borealis*. She uses the concept-first method again later in the passage:

> . . . The sun has storms that send out streams of tiny particles called electrons. Scientists call this stream the solar wind. . . .
>
> Reaching the Earth's atmosphere, the wind hits a stone wall, the magnetic field that surrounds the Earth, called the magnetosphere.

Now notice how Mary K. Corcoran (2010) starts with a metaphor before introducing the technical terms *atrium* and *ventricle* in her illustrated book *The Circulatory System*:

> The heart not only has two sides, it also has an upstairs and a downstairs. Each side has an upstairs room and a downstairs room, and each side's upstairs and downstairs are connected. The upstairs rooms are called atria (atrium, in the singular) and the downstairs rooms are called ventricles.
>
> (10)

To explain the term *aorta*, Corcoran gives the conceptual information first, then introduces the term:

> Arteries are big. All arteries have thick, elastic walls. These walls have three layers, each with lots of give so they can expand as blood passes through them. The artery you're traveling in as you leave the left ventricle is called the aorta.
>
> (16)

Concept-first teaching does take some practice and rethinking. It is easiest to do when the word you want to teach is in the form of a noun. For example, suppose you wanted to teach the word (or concept of) *colonialism*. Start by picturing it. Set up a scenario that enlists the students:

> Suppose there were a nearby school called the Elm Street School. Suppose the principal of the Elm Street School decided that they wanted to send some of their children to our school, use our classrooms, and make us sit on the floor in the hallways and bathrooms to learn. Suppose they told us that our playground games weren't as good as theirs, and they made us learn their games instead, even though we liked our own games better. Suppose they took away our playground equipment, sold it on eBay, and used the money to buy equipment for the games they played when they were at the Elm Street School. Suppose we felt that they had taken over our school, made us be like them but weren't very interested in us, and helped themselves to our favorite things. Well, there would be a name for this. We call it colonialism.

Model III: Word Components

Teaching vocabulary explicitly by breaking words down into their components—prefix, root, suffix—is essential for making sense out of polysyllabic words and for learning multiple words simultaneously. Most elementary students learn the major prefixes and suffixes (see the following lists). Very few learn the roots.

Prefixes that are usually known in elementary school include *ex-, pre-, re-, un-, dis-, non-, im-, in-, mis-, mini-,* and *maxi-*. The prefix *de-* is also on this list, but it's a little tricky, so let's give it a little more attention. *De-* can be a negative prefix, meaning *not* (*defrost, detain, defund, demystify, defuse, defeat*), *away from* (*defer, defy, delay*), or *down* (*descend, degenerate, degrade*). But it can also mean complete or intense (*deceased, delineate, detail*). Another one with more than one possible meaning is *in-*, which sometimes means *not* (*invisible, insensitive, insane, inappropriate*) and sometimes means *into* (*inject, influence, influx*).

Sometimes prefixes attach to a whole, recognizable word (*impossible, reread, enlighten, aside*), but, more often, they attach to a root, which is recognizable as part of a word that appears in many other related words[1] (*abstract, attract, distract, extract; restrict, district, constrict; reduce, induce, produce; revert, divert*).

The Power Word Kit Challenge illustrates how a profusion of words that are used in school (and business, government, and religion) are formed from a kind of "word kit" that consists of a handful of prefixes combining with a slightly larger handful of roots. See how many words your students can create on their own, adding to their lists with a partner, and then combining with larger groups. Do this at several points during the school year to celebrate vocabulary growth. Your students (and you, as well) will be unsure if something that sounds like a word is actually a word. That's where your students' dictionary skills come in handy.

The Power Word Kit Challenge

Combine the prefixes with the word roots to create 100 words.
Use only these prefixes and roots. **Do not add any letters**.
Prefixes: *a-, ab-, ad-, ap-, at-, com-, con-, de-, di-, dis-, e-, ex-, im-, in-, ob-, op-, per-, pre-, pro-, re-, sub-, sup-, trans-*
Roots: *-cess, -ceive, -clude, -duce, -fer, -gress, -ject, -mit, -pel, -plicate, -ply, -port, -pose, -scribe, -scription, -sist, -solve, -spect, -strict, -struction, -tain, -tract, -trans, -verse, -vert, -volve*

ANSWERS to the Power Word Kit Challenge (a partial list)

Beginner's List (Grades 3–5): admit, apply, attract, commit, compose, conclude, confer, congress, contract, consist, construction, contain, converse, deceive, describe, description, destruction, detract, distract, dispose, excess, exclude, expel, expose, extract, include, inject, insist, instruction, invert, involve, object, obstruction, obtain, permit, persist, prefer, prescribe, prescription, process, produce, progress, project, propel, receive, recess, reduce, refer, reject, repel, reply, report, resist, resolve, respect, restrict, retain, reverse, revolve, subject, subtract, supply, support, suppose, transfer, transmit, transport (67 words)

Advanced List (Grades 6–8): abstract, absolve, aspect, attain, compel, comply, convert, deduce, defer, deject, deport, depose, desist, detain, digress, dispel, divert, egress, emit, evolve, explicate, export, impel, implicate, imply, import, impose, induce, infer, inscribe, inscription, inverse, perceive, pertain, perverse, pervert, preclude, prospect, protract, regress, remit, replicate, retract, revert, submit, subscribe, subscription, subsist, subvert, transcribe, transcription, transgress (52 words)

Verbs turn into nouns on this list in a patterned way: *deceive, conceive, perceive,* and *receive* become *deception, conception, perception,* and *reception. Describe, transcribe,* and *prescribe* become *description, transcription,* and *prescription. Compel, impel, repel,* and *propel* become *compulsion, impulsion, repulsion,* and *propulsion.*

A Little Spelling and Pronunciation Secret

In any construction kit, specialized devices are used to ensure a good fit, and so it is with words. We call these devices connectives, and they are four of the vowels: *a, i, o, u* (rarely *e,* so we won't be discussing that). In English several morphemes are pronounced as *sh* or *zh*: -cial (*artificial, superficial, initial*), -tion (*admission, condition*), -sion (*expansion*), -cious (*conscious*), and -xious (*anxious, obnoxious*). That little syllable formed by the vowel-connective is always accented. In *English Isn't Crazy!,* Diana Hanbury King gives us this little secret, which helps us teach spelling and pronunciation: The vowels *a, o,* and *u* are strong. They are strong enough to say their own names: *vacation, occasion, promotion, commotion, explosion, exclusion, confusion.* Poor little *i* is a weak little thing with no meat on its bones. It gets the short sound when it is the connective before the *sh* or *zh*: *addition, condition, division, revision, incision* (Hanbury King, 2000).

Root of the Week is a good idea, much better than word of the day and word of the week, which result in minimal retention and minimal learning, respectively. Have your students be on the lookout for examples of this week's Latin word root in their readings, and encourage them to use words with Latin-based roots as they write. Latin-based words are found everywhere in English text, but they are found in informational (nonfiction) text even more than in fiction. This is because informational text uses a more business-like register of vocabulary, whereas fiction tends to use a more literary register.

Be patient. Expect misunderstandings. It does take some time to differentiate between words that are derived from Latin roots and those that just happen to look that way. For example, the word *mittens* is not derived from the Latin root -*miss* (to send), nor is *clue* related to the root in *conclude* or *sister* to *resist*. But with practice—lots of it—your students will start to get the feel of words that not only look alike inside, but share a common meaning because of their ancestry.

Model IV: Teach Words in Clusters

A single word in the human brain is a needle in a haystack. But if that needle were stuck to a bunch of other needles, it would be much easier to find. And if that needle could duplicate itself and attach itself to several different bunches of needles, each stashed in a different part of the haystack, finding it would be easier still. That is the theory behind teaching words in clusters.

We teach words in clusters when we teach them as part of a subject or within the real context of a story. I say *real* context because it is still teaching words in isolation if you extract a bunch of words from a story and turn them into a list. Unless you help students connect the words on the list to the story directly, you might as well be using just the kind of worksheets that are antithetical to reading–writing workshop, and for good reason. E. D. Hirsch (2013) calls the deliberate and deep study of a single academic topic *domain immersion*. Vocabulary growth is the result of domain immersion because when we focus on a topic, we hear words related to that topic repeatedly, in different contexts and forms.

We teach words in clusters when we teach words that name degrees of intensity of particular concepts. Picture the little paint samples that you get at the paint store to show you all the gradations of one color. Words do that. The concept is *angry*. At one extreme, are *enraged, livid, furious, infuriated, outraged*; at the other are *piqued* and *irritated*. Somewhere in the middle are *incensed, huffy, indignant, sore, mad*. Then, there are those other words, like *wrathful, spiteful, sore-headed*, and *tempestuous* that characterize a general personality trait, rather than a reaction to a specific provocation. Then there are metaphors: *hot under the collar, taking umbrage, breathing fire, fit to be tied, p***ed off*. When all of these words are learned together, they are "filed" together in the brain the way a color-coordinated closet is arranged for convenient access.

We teach words in clusters when we teach etymologically, showing words as branches of an ancestral family tree, as detailed in the previous model. Children learn the word *double*, which is related to *duplicate*, which is related to *diploma*, and various other words, from *doubt* to *diploid*. But, how does *diploma* fit in? What does a certificate of graduation have to do with *two-ness*, as we can perceive in the other words? Well, it turns out that the original (Greek) meaning of *diploma* is *paper folded double*. Aha!

Teach clusters of words that are related by topic (domain immersion), meaning (arrays of intensity on a concept, other words and expressions related to a concept), and structure (etymological roots).

Model V: Hypothesize and Verify

Have you ever seen a toddler calling all beverages by one name, such as juice, water, or milk? Eventually, through hearing beverages called by their proper names, she figures it out. There's a name for learning words that way. We call it narrowing. When we learn words organically, that is what we do. The first time we hear a word in a context, we guess its meaning and our guess is usually too broad. Each time we hear the word used in a different context, we (unconsciously) test our hypothesis, usually chipping away at it like a sculptor at a block of stone, until—*voila!*—no more narrowing needs to be done because we've arrived at a meaning that suits all contexts. Words get learned because, upon encountering them in context, we create a hypothesis and then verify it through repeated exposures in various contexts.

When I was a teacher, I always wanted, among other things, a source for teaching vocabulary that would let me show a series of well-written sentences that contained a targeted word in different contexts. Never finding that, I created it myself. I call it Decent Exposure, it lives on my website, www.amybenjamin.com, and you are welcome to use it in your classroom for free. There are 200 words divided into eight volumes, four volumes for middle school and four for high school. Through Decent Exposure, the words will teach themselves. Try it as a center activity, or mini-lesson.

After any of these procedures, students do need to "own" the word by using it in a meaningful, well-developed sentence that provides enough context to demonstrate understanding. The sentence should have at least eight words (more for older students), should use an action verb, and contain a visual image. The sentence should exemplify the organic use of the word. It should not be a sentence that bluntly defines the word.

I am recommending that no less than fifteen minutes every day be devoted to explicit vocabulary instruction, resulting in a net gain of three words (the targeted word, plus at least two collateral words). In addition, your students need to hear and see the words on the Academic Word List in the context of your teaching throughout the day. These two practices—explicit instruction on three words plus ongoing implicit instruction through your meaningful use of the AWL words—will grow your students' vocabulary. Through the explicit instruction, not only will your students learn words, but they will learn *word components* that will equip them with the analytical skills to figure out what unfamiliar words mean, especially multisyllabic words. In addition, your students will be picking up words from their independent reading.

If you do this, your students will come away with *at least* 540 words from explicit instruction (180 school days a year, times 3 words learned through explicit instruction of targeted *and* collateral words). If they pick up *one* of the additional incidental words that you use in the course of your explicit instruction, that brings them to 720 words a year. If they pick up *one* of the AWL words a day as a result of hearing you speak, they're up to 900 words a year. Now, if they spend twenty-five minutes reading a text in which they know 95% of the words, they've picked up one more word a day, bringing us to a grand total of 1,080 words during the school year. That rate of vocabulary growth will make a big difference, and at little expense to other instruction.

Key Points

1. Well-chosen words, thoroughly explored, magnetize other words. Applying this principle, you will end up giving your students a greater yield of words than you would with the traditional practice, where students do little more than memorize brief definitions, especially when given a list of unrelated words. It's a good idea to select words that children already know something about.
2. Various organizing principles may be used to group words: words related to one concept, words derived from one Latin root, words that name members of one category, Tier III (technical) words necessary for understanding a particular text, words that usually partner up with other words to form a predictable phrase (collocations).

3. When introducing a word, it is best to describe the concept and then name it (present the word after the students are already thinking about its meaning). Doing so increases the likelihood that the word will be remembered because it is being integrated into existing knowledge.

4. Teachers need to be mindful of abstractions. Abstractions, by their nature, are difficult or impossible to grasp unless they are supported by concrete examples.

5. Etymology illuminates meaning. While everyone teaches the basic prefixes and suffixes, we haven't paid nearly enough attention to the Latin roots that generate countless words and help us make educated guesses, recognize the meaning of internal syllables within words, and deepen our understanding of words by knowing their original meanings.

6. Full exploration of a word involves several dimensions of meaning and language, including pronunciation, spelling, grammatical forms, range of meaning, connotation (formal, technical, informal, slang, euphemistic), frequency, and collocations.

7. To provide memorable and meaningful instruction, use a combination of the five models of explicit instruction described at the end of this chapter.

Thorough exploration of a well-chosen targeted word leads to related words as "accessories." The explorations discussed in this chapter are led by the teacher, but students need to work with their new words. In the next chapter, we'll explain the what, why, and how of engaging students with games, puzzles, metacognition, and writing tasks.

Note

1 *Root*, *stem*, *base*, and *morpheme* are used interchangeably (except by those who study linguistics on a level that goes beyond our needs in this book) to refer to the un-affixed part of a word.

Bibliography

Corcoran, Mary K. (2010). *The Circulatory System*. Watertown, MA: Charlesbridge. 10.

Curtis, Christopher Paul. (1999). *Bud, Not Buddy*. New York: Delacorte Press, Random House.

George, Jean Craighead. (1972). *Julie of the Wolves*. New York: Harper's Trophy.

Hanbury King, Diana. (2000). *English Isn't Crazy: The Elements of Our Language and How to Teach Them*. Baltimore, MD: York Press. 103.

Hayakawa, S.I. and Alan Hayakawa. (1940, 1992). *Language in Thought and Action*, 5th Edition. Orlando, FL: Harcourt. 82–96.

Hirsch, E.D. (January 9, 2013). A Wealth of Words. *City Journal*. 3. The *Glossary of Education Reform: Edglossary.org/engagement*. Accessed June 10, 2016.

K.C.L. (n.d.). Crawford's Portfolio. https://kclcrawford.wordpress.com/papers-projects/william-caxton-and-the-shaping-of-written-english/. Accessed June 10, 2016.

Lobel, Arnold. (1971). *Frog and Toad Together*. New York: Harper Trophy.

Marzano, Robert J. (2004). *Building Background Knowledge for Academic Achievement*. Alexandria, VA: ASCD. 69.

Platt, Richard and Chris Riddell, illus. (1999). *Castle Diary: The Journal of Tobias Burgess*. Somerville, MA: Candlewick Press.

3

Engagement

The two previous chapters have addressed exposure and exploration, which are two teacher-centered ways of growing vocabulary through indirect and direct instruction, respectively. In this chapter and the next, we'll discuss student-centered engagements that promote true ownership of new words. The activities in these chapters conform to the principle that *learning results from problem-solving*. A substantial amount of word study time should have students solving interesting, accessible problems related to words.

What Do We Mean by *Engagement*?

Everyone believes that students should be *engaged* in what they are learning. Let's think more about what this word means, and what it should not mean. Just because students look busy does not mean that they are engaged, at least not in the way that we want them to be. I'm not going to say that children doing rote copying from a dictionary or filling in easy workbook exercises are engaged. There's a difference between being occupied and being engaged. I'm not even going to say that children listening attentively to a story are engaged. There's a difference between being engaged and being entertained.

Consider this assertion: "To enhance learning, students must be engaged in a cognitive verb" (Antonetti and Garver, 2015, 80). I would add that the cognitive verb should, if at all possible, be at the higher levels of Bloom's

Taxonomy: that is, in case you need a brief refresher, activities that call for analyzing (breaking things down), synthesizing (creating combinations that are new to the learner), and evaluating (judging something against criteria). According to Antonetti and Garver (2015, 81), engagement at a high-level thinking task in a classroom is rare. (Antonetti and Garver do not conflate on-task behavior and engagement.)

Once we accept that there is a difference between a compliant and orderly classroom and an engaged classroom, we can judge the effectiveness of our vocabulary instruction (and other instruction) and perhaps be open to some untried ideas. Antonetti and Garver (2015), as a result of thousands of class-room observations, have identified eight work conditions that qualify as meaningful engagement in a task. I've combined these eight conditions into four that apply to vocabulary learning:

1. Choice and autonomy
2. The right combination of routine and novelty
3. A safe risk-taking environment
4. A sense of authenticity and usefulness

Let's give a few examples for each of these working conditions:

1. Choice and autonomy
   Rather than having the teacher or textbook dictate the words to be learned from a given story, the children have the autonomy to go through the text and select ten words for the week. For two words a day, first, they have to hazard a guess as to the meaning of the word in context. Then, they exchange their two words with a partner, and each child either affirms the guess or changes it. Then, the children consult an appropriate dictionary to verify or modify their defini-tion. Then, they exchange again, making sure that the correct defini-tion has been written.
2. The right combination of routine and novelty
   In the word study center, children work on morphology charts (see Appendix A). The morphology charts provide routine, but the novelty is that every word morphs differently. The way the English language is built, with words coming from all directions (Greek, Latin, Scandinavian, German, other), you never know how a word is going to change its forms until you actually run it through the four columns (noun, verb, adjective, adverb).

3. A safe risk-taking environment
    Antonetti and Garver make the point that competition is only as engaging as your chance of winning. They give an example of a coach who declared that competition is a sure-fire engagement. But when asked to compete in a singing contest, he demurred. Competition is engaging, but only when voluntary. When it comes to language learning, the affective domain is very important. The learner has to feel at ease using new words, admitting to unknown words, and hazarding guesses. Any kind of negative emotion—fear of embarrassment or harsh criticism, boredom, nervousness—work against language learning. This working condition should always inform how we arrange children in groups or partnerships.

4. A sense of authenticity and usefulness
    Words are meant to be used, stretched, narrowed, and played with, not just defined and tested. We've all had the experience of looking up a particular word in a dictionary and then having to look it up again *because we didn't use it*. The human brain is teeming with bits of information and input of all kinds clamoring to get inside it. Only the information that the brain thinks is worth knowing stands a chance! That is why the repeated exposure over time (spaced retrieval) is necessary. Every new word has to "fight" for inclusion by telling the brain, "Hey, you keep hearing me! You keep reading me! Don't turn me out! Find me a place and let me stay in!"

You can easily see how the reading–writing workshop is an engagement-friendly structure. Students already have plenty of choices and routines. Ideally, they are directed to "just right" books for their reading level and given plenty of support when reading or listening to texts that challenge them. Ideally, your conference time encourages them to risk the mistakes of an adventurous learner.

So your next question might be: Do I need *all* of these working conditions to engage my students? Antonetti and Garver (2015) did find that there was a tipping point, where those classrooms having none of these conditions had no engagement; classrooms having one or two of the conditions had some engagement; but classrooms having at least half of these conditions had a very large number of engaged students and a very small number of off-task ones. So, no, you don't need all four qualities, but, yes, you do need at least two of them.

You might suspect that your reading–writing workshop is not engaging (or rigorous) enough if you are seeing the following regularly:

1. Children are answering questions or creating artifacts in which everyone's answers are the same.
2. Children are not aware of, or do not take ownership of, their own progress. They are not developing the metacognitive skill of self-evaluation.
3. Children are doing only low-level thinking tasks.

Strategy 1: Vocabulary Engagements during the Read-Aloud

We want to hold students' interest in the story during a read-aloud, so we want to keep diversions minimal. However, we don't want valuable word-learning opportunities to slip by, nor do we want unknown words to impede understanding of the story as a whole. Read-aloud time is *not* the right situation for explicit (in-depth) instruction of words, but we can certainly draw words from the read-aloud story for later instruction.

Fast-Mapping

Is there any value in hearing a word whiz by, once only, during a read-aloud? Yes and no. Hearing a word a single time does place that word somewhere in the listener's orbit. If the word is briefly clarified, or if the context is rich enough to illustrate meaning, the word flies closer in, but unless the word is used repeatedly over time following the initial exposure, it will probably be forgotten (Ebbers, 2016). Some people use the term *fast-mapping* to refer to the process of learning a word very quickly, in context, with a brief clarification. We can consider fast-mapping to have a place in word-learning, but it does not replace in-depth instruction on carefully selected words.

Susan Ebbers (2016) crystallized three main ideas from the research on how listening to a read-aloud increases vocabulary (Note: Read the entire story without stopping the first time to better ensure enjoyment and to avoid disrupting the train of thought or losing track of the main ideas of the story. During subsequent reading, stop to briefly explain or paraphrase target words.):

1. In general, reading aloud to children results in more lasting vocabulary growth if we read the book more than once in the

same week. However, this varies by grade level. Repeating the same story four times has resulted in a larger effect size in kindergarten, compared to second grade (Biemiller and Boote, in Ebbers, 2016).

2. In general reading aloud to children results in deeper and more lasting vocabulary growth if we read the book more than once in the same week AND we directly teach the meaning of targeted words by paraphrasing them or briefly defining them at point of use in the text.

3. In general reading aloud to children results in deeper, more lasting, and more productive vocabulary growth if we read the book more than once in the same week AND we directly but briefly teach target words at point of use in the text AND we follow this with interactive word study (Beck et al., in Ebbers, 2016).

Many teachers already do what is called pre-teaching vocabulary, which means that they introduce and give brief explanations of key words in an upcoming read-aloud. This could be made more engaging by having the students comb through the text first and suggest words that they need to know more about. There won't be time to address all of them, so the teacher, knowing the story, will have to select the words that are the most immediately relevant. Of course, this can happen only if the students have access to the story, which many times in a read-aloud they do not. If the students can't have the text in front of them, the teacher can still offer choice and autonomy by showing a list of a variety of words that will be met in the read-aloud and asking each child to pick one. A good way to do this is with individual white boards. That way, the teacher can get an overall look at the most popular choices.

After the read-aloud, you can introduce words that capture themes and qualities in the story, but were not actually stated in the story. For example, in any Nancy Drew mystery, there will come a time when Nancy is *suspicious*, when she faces a *dilemma*, when she makes a *hypothesis*, when she trusts her *instincts*, and when she *infers* facts based on her observations. These are words that encapsulate key points in the story and are useful in thinking, talking, and writing about it.

Strategy 2: Safari: Conquering Big Words

In a "safari" procedure, students go hunting for big game—big words, that is. Setting their sights on multisyllabic words in a text, they develop the tools for breaking big words down into known components (structural analysis).

Our safari takes place in authentic texts. We're on the lookout for multi-syllabic words (words of three or more syllables). We can forgo multisyllabic words that are very common, such as *telephone, another*, in favor of words having an easily discernible base word (word without any prefix or suffix added). We can also slide past words that are probably too infrequent or abstract in a particular grade level to be attended to right now (*notarized, acknowledgement, untraceable*). Remember that just because a child knows a multisyllabic word in an aural context does not mean she will recognize it when she sees it in a text (e.g., *understanding, happening, tremendous*). Here's what we shoot down from *The Hidden Staircase* (1930), a classic from Carolyn Keene's Nancy Drew series:

Safari Type 1: Affixed Words

1. " 'Tell me more!' the eighteen-year-old *detective* begged *excitedly*."
2. "They said that many strange, *mysterious* things had been *happening* here *recently*."
3. " 'It certainly sounds *intriguing*,' Nancy replied, her eyes dancing."
4. "*Attractive*, blond-haired Nancy was brought out of her daydreaming by the sound of the doorbell."
5. "There was a deep *affection* between the two, and Nancy *confided* all her secrets to the understanding housekeeper."
6. "Willie Wharton's *signature* was never witnessed and the attached *certificate* of acknowledgement was not notarized."
7. "Such a *procedure* on the part of the *property* owners meant trouble for her father!"
8. "They had heard untraceable music, thumps and creaking noises at night, and had seen eerie, *indescribable* shadows on walls."
9. "But after talking with my mother, they came to the *conclusion* that most of what she saw and heard could be explained by natural causes."
10. "Helen turned and gazed *pleadingly* at her friend."

Processing Device: Affixed words

Rationale: The key to tackling multisyllabic words is being able to recognize affixes (prefixes and suffixes). Table 3.1 facilitates the important metacognitive strategy of separating the familiar base word from any affixes that turn it into a multisyllabic word. It's also a good device for learning to spell affixed words.

Allow students to work in small groups or pairs to *do what they can on their own.* After they've done that, you can help them with the other examples.

TABLE 3.1 AFFIXED WORDS

Word list	Base word, if any	Meaning of base word (guess)	Dictionary meaning of base word
detective	detect		
excitedly	excite		
mysterious	mystery		
recently	recent		
intriguing	intrigue		
attractive	attract		
affection	affect		
confided	confide		
signature	sign		
certificate			
procedure	proceed		
property			
indescribable	describe		
conclusion	conclude		
pleadingly	plead		

The purpose for having them first do what they can on their own is to encourage them to discover their own intuitive knowledge about words.

Safari Type 2: Compound and Hyphenated Words (see Table 3.2)

In the same span of text, we find the following compound and hyphenated words:

blond-haired, daydreaming, doorbell, housekeeper, nutshell, railroad, tree-shaded, driveway, great-aunt

TABLE 3.2 COMPOUND AND HYPHENATED WORDS

Write the compound or hyphenated words.	Write each word that makes up the compound or hyphenated word.	Write each word that makes up the compound or hyphenated word.	Guess the meaning.	Write the dictionary meaning.

Safari Type 3: Expressions

Idioms, phrases, and metaphors are also forms of vocabulary to be reckoned with. You will probably have to help students understand that *expressions* are groups of words that have a single meaning, but it's a meaning that is based on what the words remind us of. (I'm trying to avoid the terms *literal* and *metaphorical* because those terms are too abstract for some students. Begin with the concept that some words mean what they remind us of and not what the dictionary might say. Once students understand this *concept*, you can transition from saying "just an expression" to "a metaphor.")

1. "Are you tied up on a case?"

   Explanation: Being *tied up* reminds us of being unable to pay attention to something else.

2. "'. . . ,' Nancy replied, her eyes dancing."

   Explanation: *Dancing* reminds us of being happy while doing something fun.

3. "She sat lost in thought for several minutes."

   Explanation: Being *lost* reminds us of how we feel when we are thinking so hard about something else that we almost forget where we are and what we were doing.

4. "'The story in a nutshell is this,' he began."

   Explanation: A *nutshell* reminds us of a little container.

To prompt students to do their safaris for expressions, ask them to look for groups of words (phrases) that seem strange to them, that don't seem to make sense even though they do know the meanings of the individual words in the phrase. (Define *phrase* as a piece of a sentence, or as a group of words that make sense together but do not form a complete sentence.)

Strategy 3: Sorting, Matching, Grouping, and Listing

The human brain loves to create orderly systems. Sorting, matching, and grouping activities, usually associated with early mathematical thinking, begin in preschool as children learn to observe attributes: colors, sizes, shapes, textures. List-making and word-sorting are problem-solving engagements that call for higher-level thinking (specifically, comparison-contrast and evaluation). These activities are fun and low risk, especially when done in partnerships or small groups. List-making and word-sorting activities can make the difference between fragile (easily forgettable) and durable (long-lasting) knowledge.

Picture cards are excellent for vocabulary sorting centers. There should be no text on the picture cards. That is because we want the children to generate their own observations and name what they see in their own words. When a word already labels the picture, the child is likely to default to the words in the label, overlooking other possibilities in the pictures. Also, young children who cannot read the words may be discouraged. (When children find their own categories based on attributes that they observe, that is called an *open sort*.)

Concept attainment, based on the work of Jerome Bruner (1973), is a strategy for learning the particular word or phrase that captures the common attributes of a bunch of concrete examples. (It will remind you of what I referred to in Chapter 2 as "concept first.") Students have to figure out what all of the examples have in common, describe that attribute, and then learn the name for it. The process calls for inductive reasoning. Although it takes longer than deductive reasoning (where the name of the concept is given first, along with a few examples, and then the learners are asked to supply more examples), inductive reasoning is more engaging. While deductive reasoning feels like a process of applying known principles and rules, inductive reasoning feels like a process of determining what the principles and rules actually are, based on observation of examples.

Sorting Centers

Mrs. D's third-grade class has a vocabulary sorting center for words about animals. Today's concept is the word *aquatic*. There are eight pictures, five of which conform to the concept and three of which do not (an elephant bathing in a watering hole; a cat stalking prey; a dog swimming). Sticky notes marked with "yes" are affixed to the five pictures of aquatic animals; sticky notes marked with "no" are affixed to the pictures of nonaquatic animals. The sorting has already been done in a concept attainment activity. The idea, then, is for the children to figure out what the "yes" pictures all have in common. As the groups rotate through the center, they agree on a conclusion, write it on an index card, and drop it in a box marked "The Concept." (A child who disagrees with others may write his own card, of course.) When all of the groups have rotated through, Mrs. D reads the cards. For each response, she helps the class verify whether it applies to all of the "yes" examples and, if not, why not. Then, she says: "And there's a way to describe animals that live in the water most of the time: We call them *aquatic* animals." She says: "Now let's see why our 'no' cards show pictures of animals that are not aquatic animals."

The concept attainment strategy works best under three conditions (Silver et al., 2007):

1. To avoid misleading information, your examples must clearly illustrate the concept and must represent the idea that is already familiar to the students. (Let's say your concept is deciduous trees. If students do not recognize that evergreen trees do not shed their leaves, then they will not be able to induce the concept from pictures of evergreen trees.) This is called the Principle of Conceptual Clarity. The non-examples share some characteristics with the examples, but with key differences. (A dog may know how to swim but does not spend most of its life in the water the way an aquatic animal does.)

2. A tentative hypothesis can be drawn from just two examples, and further examples confirm it. This is called the Principle of Multiple Exposures. A corollary is that your first two examples should be the most obvious, while later examples may be more subtle. (If you are doing this in a vocabulary center, then you might want to number the examples in the order you want the children to look at them.)

3. We can say that a child understands the targeted word for the concept when she can delineate the essential characteristics, discriminate between examples and non-examples, and explain her reasoning, based on criteria. This is called the Principle of Conceptual Competence. Silver et al. suggest having the child create an imaginary specimen of the concept.

The concept attainment strategy embodies both routine (in the procedure) and novelty (in the devising of an imaginary specimen). It also provides for autonomy and a safe risk-taking environment, as the children begin with obvious connections between two examples and then are given clear, if more subtle, further examples to test their hypotheses.

Types of Word Sorts

Provide manipulative learning materials (words and word components on cards, big dice, movable objects on your interactive whiteboard) in word-learning centers. Students can make lists and sort words based on any number of organizing principles:

Metacognitive: Sorts words that the student knows well, knows slightly, does not know at all.

Structural: Sorts words by structural features such as has a prefix, has a suffix, has double letters, is a compound word, and so on.

Grammatical: Sorts words according to how they can fit into frames such as:

The _____ (noun)

Words that you can add *-ing* to: (verb)

Words that answer the question *What kind?* (adjective)

Words that answer the question *In what manner?* or *How would you do that?* (adverb)

Topical: Sort words related to a given topic.

Strategy 4: Self-Set Goals and Metacognition

Self-set goals and choice are motivating and engaging. Many of the words that students need to know—the words on the Academic Word List, words generated by Latin roots, the Tier III words—are foundational to academic success, so there should be no choice about whether to learn them. But other words are nice to know, and there is no list of words that has all of them. In fact, when everyone in the class learns exactly the same words, as, say, with a workbook, no one will be hearing any words other than those. No cross-pollination. You can give students a choice about the nice-to-know words.

As they read and listen, children should have a structure for maintaining their own "Words I Like" collections. It can also be called "Words I Want to Know More About." As we've been saying, one of the not-so-good teaching habits of vocabulary instruction is to focus *entirely* on words selected *for* them. Personal collections are a step toward the lifelong habit of learning about words. This is an opportunity for students to use an age-appropriate dictionary for its intended purpose: not to play "go fetch," but to verify and refine their educated guesses they've already made about a word. So, first, they should write down their guess about their word-of-interest. Then, write the dictionary definition, preferably in their own words (another processing opportunity). For further processing, they can draw a *quick* picture and either copy a few words of the context in which they encountered the word or write a well-developed sentence according to specs (see sidebar, page 66).

A good metacognitive tool is a three-column chart headed "Strangers" (for words that the student does not know at all), "Acquaintances" (for words that the student thinks are familiar, but not fully known and not used by them yet), and "Friends" (words that the student is pretty sure she knows and has used herself in speech or writing). This is a variation on a model you may have seen before, known as the Knowledge Rating

Scale (Blachowicz et al., 2006). This graphic organizer serves as formative assessment. As you look at it, you get an idea of the words that you need to use more. Students revisit their charts periodically, noting their own progress.

Students can build vocabulary based on their own interests. Almost everyone is interested in something related to sports, animals, food, and music. Have students create illustrated glossaries, selecting words of interest from their readings (books, magazines, websites).

Look for word-learning opportunities in topics that capture popular interests, such as beloved movies, exciting sports events, trending songs—anything children may be buzzing about.

We've stressed the disengaging nature of traditional vocabulary quizzes and tests. However, with some changes in attitude about what tests are for and what they can do—by lessening the negative and punitive uses of tests—we can turn them into learning tools.

Pretesting and preparing for a test can be a way to learn and remember. As it turns out, a test is not only a measurement tool. It's a way of enriching and altering memory. Testing works this way because the test questions themselves cue the brain as to what is important and what needs to be retrieved (Under the Hood, 2014).

Carey's report (cited in Under the Hood, 2014) indicates that, without a test, we don't know what we don't know. More accurately, we think we know something because we knew it once (memorized it), but test-like engagements can tell us what we've *retained*. When it comes to vocabulary, retention is the only thing that matters. (Who cares if you memorized a word for a test, never used it again, and forgot it?)

Game-like formats that offer continuous, low-stakes feedback (such as Vocabulary.com) are effective engagements because any words that students miss "come back to haunt them" in different kinds of test questions. That the targeted word, the one that was missed previously, is re-presented in different kinds of questions, is key to learning the word by playing the game.

> Here's how it (word learning) works: The first time you see a word in context, you get clues to its meaning. Some of these clues are dead-on. Others are vague at best or even downright misleading. And since your brain has no way to tell the good from the bad, it files them all away. But see the word in context again, and the brain will take note of the clues that show up a second time. Repeat this exposure many times, and the overlapping information will be further reinforced, forming itself into a cohesive sense of the word's meaning.
>
> (Under the Hood, 2012)

Thus, forgetting (pruning out irrelevant information) helps you learn because what remains as consistent is relevant.

Strategy 5: Vocabulary and Writing

We want students to practice and show mastery of vocabulary *in their writing*. Examination of student writing should be the primary means of assessment. The words we teach should be relevant to what we are asking students to think, talk, and write about, as writing and vocabulary are inextricably linked. Though this may seem obvious, the link between the vocabulary that students are taught and their writing tasks is often missing in both instruction throughout the writing process and assessment.

Note that we are not talking about the age-old, famously ineffective practice of assigning students to use a newly met word "in a sentence." We've all seen what happens: the sentences are as short as possible, with content that has little meaning. What works better is linking the writing task to the targeted words, and then supplying a small word bank (five to eight words) that will work well in that writing task. We do not expect all of the words in the word bank to be used. The process of selecting relevant, convenient words to enhance a writing piece constitutes higher-level thinking (evaluation). Don't be surprised if doing this leads to welcome questions about how to change the form of a word to fit it into the grammatical context of a sentence. And that will lead to welcome questions about spelling.

Getting Better Sentences

You don't have to abandon the practice of having students use new words in a sentence, just to show what they mean. You can improve this practice by specifying the scope, length, and content of the sentences that would actually enhance a student's understanding of the meaning of the new word as well as build sentence-composing skills. We suggest that sentences written to showcase a newly learned word include the following:

1. Substance: The sentence should be seven to twelve words long, at least, depending on the age of the students. This is to encourage meaningful context for the targeted words.

2. Specificity: The sentence should contain a visual image. This makes the sentence more memorable by connecting an image to the targeted words.
3. Strength: The sentence should use an action verb. Action verbs enliven sentences.

Vocabulary choices vary by genre. When writing a story or poem, we emphasize language that is specific in a descriptive, imaginative way, enabling the reader to experience the story or poem through the senses. Stories and poems favor nouns that name concrete things; adjectives that produce either a visual image for the concrete things or that nail a character trait; strong, specific action verbs. Fancier, abstract words are not necessarily called for in a story or poem. Many (if not most) writers of fiction, memoir, and poetry have written masterpieces by favoring powerful short words, words that pack a punch.

The stories and poems that children read should inspire them to use new and interesting words. Let's remember that vocabulary growth includes more than just the use of previously unknown words. It also includes the use of words that were previously known receptively (in reading and listening) but not productively (in writing and speech). It includes words used in ways and forms that the student has not used before. These are engagements that transition words from "acquaintances" (partially known, or known but not used productively) to "friends" (words thoroughly known and used creatively).

Although we might not use the word, we want children to learn to write stories *cinematically*. That is, we want both the big picture (panning out) and the small details (zooming in). Different kinds of words get us there. Every writer knows the maxim of "show, don't tell." That means use words that create visuals in the reader's mind. You might think that descriptions are created through adjectives, but in fact it's the strong nouns and verbs that really do the job. As we confer with students, we can help them find the right nouns and verbs (and then, only if necessary, interesting adjectives and adverbs to modify them) to create visuals. The way the English language works, you'll find, just as the greatest writers do, that it's those one- and two-syllable words that are the most powerful and specific. Look at this passage from Gillian Cross's telling of *The Odyssey*:

While they slept, the Cicones were creeping around in the hills, gathering reinforcements. At dawn, a wild army came sweeping down from the hills, looking for revenge.

Odysseus's men were woken by the clash of spears and the rattle of chariot wheels. Leaping up in a panic, they snatched at their weapons, but it was too late to form a battle line. They had to defend themselves as best they could, fighting hand to hand all over the beach.

(18)

While we may tend to associate a word like *reinforcement* with vocabulary instruction, we should remember that strong, specific verbs like *gather, sweeping, leaping, snatched,* and zoom-in noun phrases like *clash of spears and the rattle of chariot wheels* also constitute vocabulary instruction when we are teaching story writing and poetry.

But stories and poems are not what we mean when we use the term *informational writing.* For informational writing, we need to encourage the use of two kinds of words that require instruction: generic academic words and technical words. Both of these kinds of words tend to have Latin and Greek roots.

Strategy 6: Literature and Vocabulary

Because reading–writing workshop is literature centered, we should think of the stories that children are reading and writing as vocabulary-learning opportunities in three ways:

1. The metalanguage of literature
2. Words that appear in the literature
3. Word bank charts for talking about characters, settings, and key points in the story

The Metalanguage of Literature
In the course of conversing about what they are reading and writing, students should be continuously expanding and refining words that talk about literary elements. But don't just give them a list of words and definitions. By asking the kinds of questions listed next and *responding* with the metalanguage, students will gradually learn to use these words.

1. Cue: Tell us about something exciting that happened in the story.
   Name the concept: Thank you for telling us about that *episode.*
2. Cue: Was your main character afraid of another character?
   Name the concept: Thank you for telling us about the *antagonist.*

3. Cue: Where and when does your story take place?
   Name the concept: Thank you for telling us about the *setting*.
4. Cue: What kind of feeling do you get from the setting? Why?
   Name the concept: Thank you for telling us about the *atmosphere*.
5. Cue: How does your story end?
   Name the concept: Thank you for telling us about the *resolution*.
6. Cue: What is the first important thing that happens in the story?
   Name the concept: Thank you for telling us about the *first plot point*.
7. Cue: What happens next?
   Name the concept: Thank you for telling us about the *rising action*.
8. Cue: Tell us about a conversation between two characters in the story.
   Name the concept: Thank you for telling us about the *dialogue*.
9. Cue: Who is telling us the story?
   Name the concept: Thank you for telling us about the *narrative point of view*.
10. Cue: Tell us about a character who is in only one or two chapters.
    Name the concept: Thank you for telling us about a *minor character*.

Words that Appear in the Literature

We all want to draw vocabulary words from literature because the context is already there, and teaching unfamiliar words will help with comprehension. But that doesn't mean we have to address *every* unfamiliar word, as explained earlier. The criteria for word selection explained in Chapter 6 should be considered as we decide which words to define briefly in passing, which to teach thoroughly, and which to let slide.

In keeping with workshop philosophy, we should have routines in place for having the children self-select words they want to know more about. A graphic organizer or short questionnaire asks them to identify a *limited and manageable* number of words from the literature:

A word I would like to know more about is _____ on page

_____.

Can I understand the story without knowing this word? (Yes? No?)
Have I ever heard of this word before? (Yes? No?)
Does this word remind me of any other word? If so, what word?

_____

My guess: _____
Dictionary definition: _____
Was my guess "close"? (Yes? No?)

Use these responses as formative assessment to guide your instruction, as you collect data about the following:

1. The specific words that the children select:

    How relevant are these words to the story as a whole? Do the children seem to understand that some words are more important than others?
    Which of the words that the children select should I be teaching explicitly? (Chapter 2)

2. Do I need to work more on having children recognize similarities between new and known words?
3. How accurate are their guesses? If they are having trouble with this, maybe I can encourage them to make broader guesses.

In addition to single words, we need to tend to the idioms and metaphorical expressions that characterize literary text.

Adjective Bank Charts for Talking about Literary Elements

A word bank is a simple but powerful resource. It is nothing more than a list of related words offered to students to enrich their writing, speech, and thinking. It works like an inventory. Most word banks are relatively short—a handful of words that we think students already know. Typically they are rather narrow in scope, aligned to whatever subject the class is writing about. In reading–writing workshop, where children are selecting their own subject within a genre, some teachers don't know how to use word banks.

What I am suggesting is an *adjective bank*, one that acts as a reusable go-to for writing for describing three elements of literature: character, setting, and plot. I call it an adjective bank *chart* because I would like it to be on permanent classroom display, year after year in the elementary and middle schools where reading–writing workshop is practiced (and where it isn't). As you look it over, you will note that your students do already know a few of the adjectives quite well, they might be "acquainted" with some others, and they have no knowledge of some. This variety of familiarity with the words on the chart is the point. I designed the charts this way so that all students would have some easy access as well as substantial room for growth.

I realize that you will be tempted to teach all the words on the charts all at once. I believe that a better approach is to proceed slowly, trusting that, over time and with repeated exposure to the charts, students will eventually absorb all of the words. Because they did so slowly and through association with literature, they will remember the words better than they would have with a blast of explicit instruction of multiple words at once.

Encourage students to learn more about the words they already know a little about. Have them share with each other the words they have chosen to use in their writing. The theory is that just by seeing the charts over and over, by sorting through them in search of words that describe their literature, and by sharing their findings, they will transform words that are strangers into acquaintances, acquaintances into friends.

There are three adjective bank charts for character traits, setting descriptions, and plot points (all from Vocaulary.com). Start using this chart in grade 3, or even before that if you couple the words with simple visuals.[1]

Character Adjectives Chart: addled, afraid, agitated, ambivalent, annoyed, antagonistic, anxious, apprehensive, baffled, belligerent, bewildered, boastful, bored, calm, cautious, concerned, confident, confused, curious, dejected, despondent, detached, determined, discouraged, ecstatic, elated, embarrassed, enthusiastic, excited, foolish, fortunate, frantic, friendly, frustrated, furious, grateful, helpful, helpless, hopeful, hostile, humiliated, hurried, inadequate, independent, introspective, insecure, interested, intrigued, intuitive, involved, irate, jittery, lighthearted, lucky, mischievous, mixed-up, moody, mystified, nervous, optimistic, overwhelmed, perplexed, puzzled, proud, relieved, resentful, responsible, satisfied, scared, secure

Setting Adjectives Chart: active, ancient, awful, bare, blighted, business-like, bustling, charming, cheerful, cheerless, claustrophobic, contemporary, creepy, crowded, dangerous, dark, depressing, deserted, desolate, dirty, dismal, dreary, eerie, empty, fancy, glittering, God-forsaken, historic, homey, ideal, industrious, inviting, lively, lush, luxurious, magical, military, modern, mysterious, oppressive, opulent, ornate, picturesque, plain, pristine, quaint, ramshackle, romantic, rural, rustic, scenic, shadowy, splendid, strange, suburban, sunny, traditional, tropical, urban, unearthly, uninviting, unsanitary, wild, wintry, wondrous, woodsy

Plot Adjectives Chart (these adjectives describe how the reader finds the story at particular points—remember that we are focusing on the reader's reactions here, not the character's actions): action-packed, bittersweet, comforting, complicated, confusing, depressing, descriptive, detailed, emotional, exciting, familiar, funny, gloomy, gory, grim, heartwarming, hilarious, hopeful, humorous, intriguing, ironic, intense, joyful, memorable, odd, ominous, painful, perplexing, philosophical, pleasing, predictable, puzzling, realistic, romantic, sad, scary, shocking, surprising, suspenseful, thrilling, tragic, unclear, unexpected, unforgettable, unnatural, unusual, vague, violent, vivid, wild

One fast and efficient way for students to learn and practice vocabulary independently is through a computer-assisted language learning resource called Vocabulary.com. Vocabulary.com uses an adaptive learning strategy that feeds the learner the particular words that she needs to master, providing a variety of question types (including visuals and multiple contexts).

Vocabulary.com technology uses the data generated by student responses to questions on given words. This system, called item response theory (IRT), allows *only* appropriate questions to be shown to the learner because it "knows how" to zero in to their skill level, based on their responses to previous questions. It is perfect for your word study center.

Using the principle of spaced repetition (a.k.a. spaced retrieval), Vocabulary.com re-asks questions, in different ways, about words that the learner got wrong. I like to say that the words you get wrong with Vocabulary.com keep coming back to haunt you, until you get them right (and get them right more than once). This technique, called "retrieval practice," has been shown through the research (Karpicke and Reedier, 2008; Paul 2011, in Zimmer) to be very effective in getting words to *get learned and stay learned*.

The designers of Vocabulary.com know that humans learn words when the words are repeated in multiple contexts and forms. Their pool of questions is vast enough to present the learner who needs work on a word with questions that go beyond shallow knowledge of brief definitions. There are questions on synonyms, antonyms, sentence completions, matching a word to a visual, and identifying examples.

Vocabulary.com also has a dictionary that supplies thorough but comprehensible definitions, fully developed through examples and anecdotes that connect the student to the word. (It also gives audio pronunciations, morphological forms, frequency data, and example sentences from a variety of sources, including news publications, technical fields, and contemporary and classical literature.)

Students become intensely engaged in Vocabulary.com because it has the features of a game. It is fast moving, low risk but challenging, capable of rewarding success with points, badges, achievements, even competitions with other participating schools.

You can input any set of vocabulary words in a matter of seconds, but Vocabulary.com already has chapter-by-chapter lists for most of the books in your guided reading bins for grades 4 and up. It also is already loaded with each subset of the Coxhead Academic Word List and words derived from particular Latin word roots. So you can synchronize your reading–writing workshop to Vocabulary. com easily.

Key Points

1. Engagement and compliance are not the same. The kind of engagement we are looking for provides the sense of accomplishment that results in completing a challenge that is personally meaningful.
2. Vocabulary development should be included in read-aloud time. This may be done by pre-teaching one or two key words prior to the read-aloud or by stopping briefly to clarify words as you read. After the read-aloud, you can introduce words that explain or describe key ideas and character traits.
3. Students can conquer multisyllabic words by searching them out in authentic text and then learning the tools for breaking them down (structural analysis).
4. Organizational activities such as list-making, word-sorting, and concept attainment appeal to the human brain's pattern-finding tendencies. Finding patterns and making groupings facilitate word retrieval.
5. By using personal word journals and other metacognitive tools, students will grow their vocabularies by selecting and monitoring words of their choice. Using a metacognitive tool that we are calling Strangers, Acquaintances, Friends, students can track their own progress.
6. Students should always be stretching their vocabularies as they work on a writing task. We should include word banks with suggested vocabulary in directions for writing tasks. A breakdown of words appropriate for various informational topics is included in this chapter.

Note

1 The words on these three charts have been inputted into Vocabulary.com as vocabulary lists titled Character Adjectives Chart, Setting Adjectives Chart, and Plot Adjectives Chart.

Bibliography

Antonetti, John V. and James R. Garver. (2015). *17,000 Classroom Visits Can't Be Wrong.* Alexandria, VA: ASCD. 80.

Biemiller, Andrew and C. Boote. (2006). Cited in Ebbers, Susan. (2016). *Vocabulogic.* http://vocablog-plc.blogspot.com/2011/05/how-to-read-aloud-to-children-to.html. Accessed June 10, 2016.

Blachowicz, Camille L.Z., Peter Fisher, Donna Ogle and Susan Watts-Taffe. (2006). Vocabulary: Questions from the Classroom. *Reading Research Quartrely*, 41(4), 524–539.

Bruner, Jerome. (1973). *Going Beyond the Information Given.* New York: Norton.

Cross, Gillian and Neil Packer, illus. (2012). *The Odyssey.* London, England: Walker Books.

Ebbers, Susan. (June 10, 2016). *Vocabulogic.* http://vocablog-plc.blogspot.com/p/vocabulary-brief.html. Accessed June 10, 2016.

Keene, Carolyn. (1930). *The Hidden Staircase.* New York: Grosset and Dunlap.

Neff, Linda S. (1956). Learning Theories Website. Jerome Bruner on concept attainment strategies. https://jan.ucc.nau.edu/lsn/educator/edtech/learningtheorieswebsite/bruner.htm. Accessed June 10, 2016.

Silver, Harvey F., Richard W. Strong and Matthew J. Perini. (2007). The Strategic Teacher: Selecting the Right Research-Based Strategy for Every Lesson (Chapter 7: Concept Attainment). Alexandria, VA: ASCD.

Under the Hood. (April 9, 2012). *Can Forgetting Help You Learn?* http://www.vocabulary.com/articles/under-the-hood/can-forgetting-help-you-learn/. April 9, 2012. Accessed June 10, 2016.

Under the Hood. (September 16, 2014). *New Study Shows We Learn Best When We First Fail.* http://www.vocabulary.com/articles/under-the-hood/new-study-shows-we-learn-best-when-we-first-fail/. September 16, 2014. Accessed June 10, 2016.

Zimmer, Benjamin. (n.d). Vocabulary.com. The Science of Learning. Thinkmap, Inc.

4

Energy

Reading–writing workshop is an energetic classroom model, which is why so many students, teachers, parents, and administrators like it so much. The energy comes from connectedness, motivation, engagement, confidence, building on continual successes, and just a pervasive sense of joy about the whole enterprise of going to school and learning. Energy is not just nice to have as we help students grow their ability to use language. Energy is essential.

In her book *Reaching English Language Learners in Every Classroom: Energizers for Teaching and Learning* (Routledge, 2012), Debbie Arechiga says that vocabulary is not just a piece of the pie of literacy instruction; it is "the crust on which the entire pie is constructed" (165). "It's because vocabulary does so much to stimulate academic success that it's one of our Energizers. V is for vocabulary, and the academic vigor and victory it promotes!" (165).

Keep your reading–writing workshop energy level up by making sure these elements of seamless vocabulary instruction are in place:

1. As the teacher, your own vocabulary is extremely important. Get in the habit of using the words you want students to learn. Repeat, recast, reword, and summarize your own messages, using a variety of words meaning the same thing. Remember that, for many students, you are their main source of academic and business-like Standard English. Hearing the language comes first, before speaking, reading, and writing.

2. **Use your read-aloud as vocabulary opportunities**. It may seem contradictory for me to advise stopping to briefly define "stranger words" during a read-aloud, since I've inveighed against brief definitions so many times already. But there's a difference between clarifying a word by briefly defining it without breaking the stride of a story during a read-aloud and thinking that your brief definition serves as all the vocabulary instruction your students need.

3. **Independent reading is valuable, if gradual, vocabulary-learning time**. The reading–writing workshop teacher believes in "just right" books, those with enough challenge to allow the reader's skills to grow (including vocabulary) but not so much of a challenge that the reader loses interest and feels defeated. And when students are given the opportunity to talk about their readings, help them reach for new words. There are lists of adjectives later in this chapter.

4. **Select words carefully and purposefully for explicit instruction, and when you decide to teach a word, do it *thoroughly***. Teach word roots again and again and again. Nagy and Anderson (1984) say, "For every word known by a child who is able to apply morphology and context, an additional one to three words should be understandable" (in Arechiga, 2012, 177). Select vocabulary words that are going to be useful, especially because you can tie them in to current topics in your classroom. "Accessorize" targeted words by adding words related by topic, meaning, and structure (etymology). Use visuals, inductive reasoning (concept attainment), and yes/no questions about the targeted words as much as possible. And don't let the word wither away after you've taught it. Keep it alive by using it in various forms and contexts. If you find that you can't do that, ask yourself why you chose this word to teach explicitly. Maybe it wasn't useful enough.

5. **Teach word-learning strategies**. Encourage students to hypothesize a word's meaning *before* looking it up. If a sentence and surrounding sentences do not offer up enough information to hypothesize about a given word, teach them to ask broader questions: *Do I think this word means something that is good or bad? Does this word look like any other word I know that might make sense in this context? What is one definition for this word that I know* can't *be right? How do I know?*

6. **Be curious and playful about words**: eponyms, jargon, neologisms, borrowings, dialect, generalized trademarks, eggcorns, shibboleths, spoonerisms, malapropisms, clipped words, toponyms, unpaired words, even nonsense words; these are all "words about words" that delight us, just because we're human and humans love words and

wordplay. (See the end of this chapter for explanations and examples of words about words.)

Games and Puzzles

Son: *Guess what? I got to spend fifteen minutes playing a computer game at school today.*

Mom: *Oh, great. What were you learning with the game?*

Son: *(sighs) Mom, you don't learn with games. You just play.* (Hiller, 2015)

We can never underestimate the role that fun plays in learning language. Children begin playing with words as toddlers, if not before that. Fun is a natural element in language learning. It helps us stretch words and remember them. And it creates a positive classroom community, so important for language learning. Developmental psychologist Lev Vygotsky believed that play "serves a fundamental role in the child's development, because it creates a zone of proximal development in which the child always behaves beyond his 'average'" (in Lantolf, 1997). In this chapter we will describe how games, puzzles, and creative dramatics support learning vocabulary in reading–writing workshop.

Vocabulary games and puzzles are fun and engaging. They energize the learning process by building classroom community and providing multimodality learning, spaced repetition, flexibility, retrieval, speed, and even spelling reinforcement.

When we play word games and solve puzzles that draw from the words we've learned—either thoroughly or partially—we are reminded of words that might otherwise have faded through the process of neural pruning (see the "Forgetting the Forgettable" sidebar). "Games and puzzles provide the repeated exposure and spaced repetition that convert fragile knowledge to permanent knowledge" (Under the Hood, 2015).

The more time you spend searching for a word or name inside your brain, the greater the chances that the word or name will be remembered in the future. This phenomenon makes the case against the immediate gratification of Googling information before we've given ourselves a chance to pull it out of our heads (when we know it's in there somewhere). Given the ease and habit of grabbing for our devices in mid-conversation (thereby curtailing conversation itself), the old-fashioned way of retrieving information (a.k.a. *thinking*) is a hard sell. Unless we can make it fun.

You probably already have lots of word games and puzzles in your learning centers, and you probably already engage the whole class in word-generating activities that feel like games. (Flashcards are drills, not games.)

Forgetting the Forgettable

The human brain loves to learn words, but it is efficient—too efficient to hold on to words and facts that it does not use. We "make room" in our brains through "neural pruning," a scientific name for forgetting. But neural pruning is a narrower concept than plain old forgetting, like forgetting where we laid our scissors or an in-law's birthday. Neural pruning serves the cognitive purpose of shedding unused information so that we can focus on that which is actually being used. Games and puzzles, by recycling words, guard against neural pruning of words, as if words are saying to the brain, "Hey, we're here! Don't neural prune us!" With enough reminders of the existence of particular words, those words establish permanent places in our brains.

Five Types of Games and Puzzles

1. **Brainstorming:** Brainstorming promotes rapid generation of words and flexibility about word meanings. Commercially available games are Taboo and Scattergories. You can use A-to-Z charts, and variations of the idea, to challenge students to think of words relevant to a given topic that start with each letter of the alphabet.

2. **Crossword Puzzles and Variations:** Never underestimate the learning power of crossword puzzles. They promote flexibility in thinking about words, reinforce spelling patterns, provide a structure for reviewing newly learned and previously learned words, and often involve thinking about the differences among synonyms that could reasonably satisfy the clue but don't fit into the puzzle (evaluating choices). Unlike "getting a worksheet done," there's something exhilarating about finishing a crossword puzzle. You can easily customize and create crossword puzzles, and your students can as well. Crossword puzzles can include various kinds of ways of knowing words: definitions, synonyms, antonyms, examples, abbreviations. And your students could turn into crossword hobbyists, with lifelong rewards. Crossword puzzles are convenient, as you don't need to spend time explaining directions.

3. **Physical Games:** Call upon your creative-thinking powers to incorporate word-learning skills into your favorite get-up-and-move-around classroom games. Here's a starter kit of ideas:

   - Vocabulary Seven-Up: You make up two sets of index cards, one with vocabulary words or word roots; the other with definitions, or sentences with blanks, or examples of words based on a word root. As the seven children who are "up" go around the room pushing their classmates' thumbs down, they drop off one of the cards. The children who are tapped can get their turns at going "up" only by matching the word that was placed on their desks with the corresponding cards that are held by the children who tapped them.

- Vocabulary Simon Says: Enhance the language-learning capacity of the game by having Simon give commands that use vocabulary words. You can't do this with all of Simon's commands, but when it works, you will be strengthening word-retrieval muscles by linking a word to a physical action.
- Vocabulary Statues: This game is usually played by having children dance to music and then freeze when the music stops. Replace the dancing with stand-in-place movements (to reduce chaos), and replace the music with your reading aloud of a text. Children freeze when they hear any one of several interesting words that you have written on the board before reading and that they will hear at some point in the text.
- Secret Adverb Act-Out: Write various adverbs on cards and put them into a fishbowl. "It" picks out an adverb and acts it out in this context: "He joined the team _____ly." The class has to guess the adverb. To involve more children, several can act out the secret adverb at once.
- Vocabulary Baseball: A variation on the "classroom baseball diamond" game that you probably know. This time, pitch words and hit definitions.

4. **Dictionary Games:** Create scavenger hunts that send students into the nooks and crannies of dictionary entries (alternate spellings, etymology, morphological forms, uncommon meanings of a given word, etc.).

5. **Word Components Games:** There are two kinds of word components games: match-ups and listing.

- For the match-up type of game, you set up a variety of pieces, some of which are prefixes and some of which are roots. (You can also include suffixes, but that complicates things because adding suffixes often entails a spelling change. Unless you want the match-up game to be *about* the spelling change, it's best to use just prefixes and roots.)
- There are various ways to make the pieces, but you should always use two different colors for the prefixes and roots. For children to play at their desks, use index cards. You can also use

large dice, marked with the prefixes on one die and roots on the other. For students to move around the room, matching up to create "human words," use paper plates hanging around student's necks, like ID tags. To do the match-ups on a board, use magnets.

- The following is a handy list of prefixes and roots that, when combined to form words, do not require a spelling change:

Prefixes: *a-, ad-, ap-, at-, bi-, com-, con-, de-, dis-, e-, en-, ex-, im-, per-, pre-, pro-, re-, retro-, sup-, trans-, uni-*

Roots: *-active, -ception, -ceive, -cess, -clude, -clusive, -cur, -cycle, -duce, -duct, -fer, -ference, -fine, -flect, -flict, -form, -formation, -fuse, -gress,- gressive, -herent, -ject, -late, -lateral, -mand, -mise, -miss, -mission, -mit, -mote, -munity, -novate, -pact, -peal, -pel, -plicate, -plain, -plicit, -plode, -ply, -port, -pose, -position, -pulsive, -putation, -quest, -scription, -spective, -scribe, -scription, -spire, -tend, -tended, -tense, -tension, -tention, -tort, -tortion, -tract, -treat, -tail, -verse, -version, vert, -vision, -volve*

- For the listing kinds of games, students are given a prefix or root and compete to list as many words as they can in a short amount of time.

Most word games and puzzles will not teach unknown words. Their value lies in allowing for repetition and retrieval, which in the long run makes the words more available in the brain. For English language learners, who have not developed the intuition to know if a word "sounds right," the word games and puzzles can reinforce the auditory patterns of English,

Some Words about Words

Part of your skill as a teacher of words is to tell their stories. By giving students the backstories about words with interesting pedigrees, you are not only helping them remember the words, but you are also helping them make order out of what seems like the chaos of some of the strange-sounding words that have set up shop in the far-flung English lexicon. Here's a starter kit for your collection of word stories:

1. In 1880, a group of Irish tenant farmers rose up against their British landlords, demanding a reduction in their rents. When the rent collector, a man named Captain Charles Boycott, refused to yield, the tenant farmers enacted a new kind of protest: they would band together to refrain from harvesting crops (for their British landlords).

This form of nonviolent but effective form of protest became known as a *boycott*.

According to Greek mythology, Narcissus was a man of great beauty, especially according to himself. Many women and nymphs, including Echo, tried to gain his affection, but he was so taken with his own reflection in the lake that he ignored all admirers, fell in the water, and drowned. Hence, we have the word *narcissism*, meaning excessive (and ridiculous) self-love. As for Echo, she was so grief-stricken from the whole thing that she faded into the mountains, leaving nothing but her voice, which is how we get the word *echo*.

There's a name for words like these. We call them *eponyms*. An eponym is a word that is named after a person, real or fictitious. Many eponyms come from Greek mythology and many are metaphorical phrases. Some still bear their status as proper nouns, such as *Achilles' heel*, *Scrooge*, *Caesar salad*, and *Doppler effect*. Others have lost their capital letters, and as they have blended into the language, we know the word only and we no longer associate it with the person from whom it derives: *mesmerize, sandwich, wattage*.

2. The *Frank and Ernest* books by Alexandra Day are about how the two animal/human characters learn about the fields of truck driving (*Frank and Ernest on the Road*), baseball (*Frank and Ernest Play Ball*), and running a diner (*Frank and Ernest*). In *Frank and Ernest on the Road*, they become real gear jammers and learn to say things like, "Here I am behind the roulette wheel. I'm releasing the Emma Jesse brake," and "I hope a bear on rubber pulls him over before he buys the farm." There's a name for the way Frank and Ernest are using words. We call words that are used in a specialized way *jargon*. The informality of jargon makes it like slang; the narrowness and specificity of its use makes it like technical language. Metaphors and acronyms are often used in jargon. In the preceding examples, the "roulette wheel" is a metaphor for the steering wheel, the "bear on rubber" is a metaphor for a police car, and "buys the farm" is a metaphor for getting killed in a wreck. We all use jargon of one kind or another. Jargon creates a bond among members within a discourse community: if you can use it like the other members do, then you are accepted as a true member. If you stumble, mispronounce, or fail to use it when others do, then you are branded as a nonmember. Children love secret languages, which is, in a way, what jargon is. They probably know lots of sports jargon, boy and girl scouts jargon, and maybe even the jargon of your school (see *acronym, shibboleth*).

3. The noun *troll* still refers to the nasty fictitious creature that lurks under the bridge, but today, *troll* is used as a noun or verb to refer to a nasty person who posts insulting comments online, or the act of doing so. We have become used to hearing the word *door-buster* about sales on *Black Friday*. You might know someone who *vapes* instead of smokes, and who purchases *vaping* supplies from a local *vapologist*.

    There's a name for these new words and phrases (or, new uses for existing words). We call them neologisms. New words are always popping up, sometimes sticking around long enough to find a place in a new dictionary, sometimes disappearing like bubbles. A profusion of neologisms comes along with new technologies and fads. As we need new names for new things, we don't just make them up out of the air. We recombine words (*emoticon*) creating something called a *portmanteau*. We probably know that *emoticon* is a portmanteau formed from the words *emotion* and *icon*, but older portmanteau words just blend in as if they've always been there: *smog* (smoke and fog), *newscast* (news and broadcast), *brunch* (breakfast and lunch), and *sitcom* (situation comedy). Give students "word licenses" to make up portmanteaus and other neologisms. Anyone can create language and use their own words in informal situations. Who knows? It could catch on and end up in the dictionary someday. In illuminating all of the avenues through which sounds take on meaning, we demystify language and make children aware of their ownership of the *living* language.

4. The English language is amalgamated, consisting of what we call "borrowings" from many other languages. Sometimes, whole fields of knowledge use words "borrowed" from other languages. Words in the field of music, for example, are "loan words" from Italian. If any of your students practice Russian ballet, they are learning English words taken from French. The foods we eat and the ways we prepare them are named from words from all over the world.

5. The word *borrowing* in this context is ironic, as it is what we call a *misnomer*, a misleadingly named word. We have no intention of "returning" any of our "borrowed" words. Other examples of misnomers are *glow worms*, which are not worms; *koala bears*, which are not bears; peanuts and coconuts, which are not nuts; and *catgut*, which is actually made from the intestines of sheep.

6. Dialects are varieties of a language. We often think of dialects as being mainly about pronunciation, but they are also characterized by

a few differences in grammar and informal vocabulary. Your students may refer to sweet carbonated beverages as *soda, soda pop, pop,* or even *Co-Cola* (a common Texas-ism), depending on their dialect, which depends on the geographical region in which they live now, or where they lived previously. Certain words are telltale signs of a dialect. For example, if you say *Frisco* and you're in San Francisco, any city native will mark you for a tourist. Same goes for the unstreetwise person in New York who refers to Sixth Avenue as *Avenue of the Americas* (which is what the sign says, but *never* what a New Yorker says). And, you guessed it, there's a name for that. A word or phrase that marks the user as an outsider or insider is called a *shibboleth.* You'll find that children get very excited to share dialectical differences, and you can use their energy to help them respect diversity.

7. Have you ever heard anyone ask for a *Band-Aid*, a *Kleenex*, a *Q-tip*, *Scotch tape* or some *Bubble Wrap*? Ever dressed a baby in a *Onesie*? prepared dinner in a *Crock-Pot*? Ever moisten your lips with *Chap-Stick*? These are all trademarked product names that have been treated, over time and wide use, like generic words. There's a name for words like these. We call them generalized trademarks, and a few others are *Dumpster, Laundromat, Flip Phone, Dry Ice, Cellophane, Trampoline,* and even *videotape.* Generalized trademark words are fun and surprising, but the name for them, *generalized trademark,* could use an upgrade to a snappier neologism. Maybe your students can think of one?

8. Ever hear someone say that something was for all *intensive purposes*, making a *mute point*, or *wetting their appetite*? These expressions kind of make sense, but they are mistakes—mis-hearings of the original idioms *intents and purposes, moot point,* and *whetting the appetite.* Some people call these mistaken expressions *folk etymology,* but there's a better name for them: we call them *eggcorns.* The word *eggcorn* is the result of a mistaken hearing of *acorn. Eggcorn* is so apropos that it has become more than an example of something; it has become the name for the thing itself. And there's even a name for *that*: we call it an *autological* word, which means a word that belongs to the category that it also names. Your students don't need to know the word *autological*, but surely they will be tickled by *eggcorn* and the other eggcorns.

9. Is it roaring with pain or pouring with rain? Are we waving the sails or saving the whales? Should you go and shake a tower or take a shower? Chewing the doors or doing the chores? We've all made these hilarious reversals, accidents of speech with unintended

comical effects. There's a word for that, an eponym, in fact. It's called a spoonerism, named for the eccentric William Archibald Spooner, whose lectures on ancient history and philosophy at Oxford College in the nineteenth and twentieth centuries regaled his students and embarrassed him no end. Sometimes, as in the preceding examples, spoonerisms maintain the integrity of actual words in English, even though they make little sense. Other spoonerisms end up with nonsense words, as in the legendary story by the radio personality F. Chase Taylor (a.k.a. Colonel Stoopnagle).

10. British playwright Richard Sheridan wrote a play called *The Rivals* in which a character named Miss Malaprop tried to show off by using polysyllabic words but did so incorrectly, to comic effect: "Why, murder's the matter! Slaughter's the matter! Killing's the matter!—but he can tell you the perpendiculars." And that is why mistakes like these are called by the eponym *malaprops.*

11. Every day, we might hear the words *fan, burger, deli, flu, exam, fridge, gym,* and *gas.* These words are shortened forms of *fanatic, hamburger, delicatessen, influenza, examination, refrigerator, gymnasium,* and *gasoline.* There's a name for these abbreviations that are treated as full words. We call them clipped words. Clipped words have an informal feel to them. You can use them as examples of the difference between informal and formal tone. (*Plane* is less formal than *airplane*). Some original words that have become clipped have almost disappeared in the language. No one says *necktie* and *brassiere* anymore. We use the clipped forms *tie* and *bra.* For other clipped words, the original form has gone completely out of use: *movie* for *moving pictures; bus* for *omnibus.* For others, the original form would be uncomfortably formal: *typo* for *typographical error; memo* for *memorandum.*

12. The first psychiatric hospital in London was known as bedlam, a shortened form of its full name, St. Mary's of Bethleham. Today, the word *bedlam* is a synonym for *pandemonium.* Some words are named after people (eponyms); others are named after places. We call the latter words toponyms. The *tuxedo* is named for Tuxedo, New York; the *marathon* is named for Marathon, a city in Greece; and, yes, *turkey* is from Turkey, and *china* is from China.

13. A cruel person can be called ruthless, but a kind person is not called ruthful. When you recover from being discombobulated, overwhelmed, disgruntled, or disheveled, you are not *combobulated, whelmed, gruntled,* or *sheveled.* There's a name for words like these, but it's not very technical. We simply call them unpaired words. Others are *insipid, dejected, feckless, inane, inept,* and *untoward.*

Unpaired words beg the question: Why? The answer, if you consider this an answer, is that words can be finicky. Like people, most words like to follow rules. That makes them agreeable and easy to use. And if a word is easy to use, its chances of survival are good. But some words are just plain stubborn. Or weird.

Key Points

1. In your enthusiasm for the many exciting components of reading–writing workshop, don't forget that word-learning is fun and rewarding.
2. Games and puzzles that students find enjoyable are an important element in vocabulary instruction. Most games and puzzles are good reinforcers and reminders. They generally are not the best way to introduce words.
3. Learning a host of "words about words" helps students understand language change and variation.

Bibliography

Arechiga, Debbie. (2012). *Reaching English Language Learners in Every Classroom: Energizers for Teaching and Learning.* New York: Routledge. 165. www.etymonlilne.com.

Day, Alexandra. (1994). *Frank and Ernest on the Road.* New York: Scholastic.

Hiller, A. Spires. (September/October, 2015). Digital Game-Based Learning: What's Literacy Got to Do With It? *Journal of Adolescent and Adult Literacy,* 59(2), 125–130.

Lantoff, J. (1997). The function of language play in the acquisition of L2 Spanish. In W. R. Glass and A.T. Perez-Leroux (Eds.), *Contemporary Perspectives On The Acquisition of Spanish* (pp. 3–24). Somerville, MS: Cascadilla Press.

Under the Hood. (March 2, 2015). *For SAT Prep, List-Learning Starts With List Building.* http:www.vocabulary.com/articles/under-the-hood/list-learning-starts-with-list-building/

Appendix A
Balanced Literacy and Reading–Writing Workshop

A balanced literacy program incorporates features of whole language, which relies on immersion in quality literature to implicitly teach the skill of reading, and the phonics approach, which relies on letter-sound relationships and introduces children to texts having language that corresponds to the letter combinations they have learned to decode. No experts on reading pedagogy side with either immersion or phonics alone. The balanced literacy approach represents a truce in what educators have termed the "reading wars," a debate that has been going on for decades.

The reading–writing workshop is a component of a balanced literacy curriculum. In the workshop, the children practice and reflect upon what they have learned in the other components. The breakdown of these other components, according to Barb Golub, global literacy consultant and former staff developer with the Teachers College Reading and Writing Project led by Lucy Calkins, is as follows.

The Read-Aloud: The teacher reads quality literature aloud to the class. The students listen only. (They do not follow along in their own copies of the book being read aloud.) This component of instruction creates a positive feeling about reading. It introduces students to words that they might not be able to handle on their own in books that are the level that they can read independently. And it models the intonation, pauses, pacing, and emphasis that makes text come alive. Although read-aloud time should be focused on the story and not on discreet skills, the teacher can stop to highlight certain interesting words and have brief interactions about them with the students.

Shared Reading: In shared reading, the teacher and the students have the same book, and the students have their eyes on the text as the teacher reads aloud and explains the strategies necessary to comprehend. The strategies often involve vocabulary, which include:

1. Helping students recognize prefixes and how they alter the meaning of the base word.
2. Helping students recognize suffixes and how they allow the base word adapt to its grammatical role in the sentence.
3. Helping students recognize compound words.

4. Determining if there are sufficient contextual clues to discern the meaning of a word, and if not, whether they can make educated guesses about the word: *Does it represent something good or something bad? Is it a living thing? Does it exist indoors or outdoors? Can it be done by a human? Can it be seen? heard? touched?* and so on. During shared reading time, students who are skillful readers may also read aloud and explain their thinking.

Guided Reading: The teacher arranges students with similar reading abilities into small groups. Students are given books at their instructional level, that is, a level that is challenging without being frustrating. As the groups are reading, the teacher circulates, helping each group with accessible skills and strategies. Vocabulary always plays a large role in any readability formula and reading assessment, so we can assume that students in the same reading groups share similar vocabulary strengths and weaknesses.

Word Study (a.k.a. Word Work): This is where students work on engaging activities and solve interesting problems related to words. This includes vocabulary, especially word-awareness skills such as understanding word components (prefixes, suffixes, roots, compound words), synonyms and antonyms, morphology (grammatical forms of words), and spelling.

The Read-Aloud, Shared Reading, Guided Reading, and Word Study sessions enable students to read and write in a workshop. The workshop begins with a mini-lesson, called a Teaching Point. The mini-lesson explains and models something that skillful readers and/or writers do, for example:

Good readers reread, slow down, or seek help, when they don't understand something.
Good readers visualize.
Good readers listen in their heads as they read.
Good readers recognize how prefixes change the meaning of the base word.
Good readers break multisyllabic words down.
Good readers understand that they don't have to know the meaning of every single word in the text as they read.
Good readers recognize that sometimes the author keeps secrets.
Good readers pay attention to punctuation.
Good writers think about their readers, and they do everything they can to be kind to their readers.
Good writers begin sentences with capital letters and end sentences with end punctuation so that their readers can see where a sentence begins and ends.

Good writers arrange ideas in paragraphs so that their readers can see where main ideas begin and end.

Good writers strive to find the perfect words so that their readers can visualize, know the details, and not have to read unnecessary words.

Good writers revise so that their readers can get the best version.

The writing workshop may also include interactive writing, in which the class collaborates on a writing piece that everyone can see, as the teacher cues the students and forms their ideas into properly written sentences.

While the students are reading and writing independently and quietly sharing and helping each other in pairs, the teacher holds conferences with individual students and keeps records of their progress and needs. Before class ends, students are given time to shape and share what they are working on and what they have learned.

Here are a few of the differences between reading–writing workshop and traditional classrooms:

In a traditional classroom, literacy instruction emanates from a basal reader (a.k.a. *reading series*). The basal reader comes with a sequential set of skills that are presented to the students as worksheets, study questions, and "suggested activities." The class works through the basal reader, from page 1 to the end, eliminating or supplementing a selection here and there at the teacher's discretion. Usually, students are divided into three or four ability-based reading groups that meet with the teacher to do round-robin reading while the other children do "seatwork" independently.

In a reading–writing workshop, there is more self-selected, independent reading. Also, students read in pairs and small groups. The reading–writing workshop has a read-aloud component as well.

The literature in the basal reader has vocabulary that the publisher thinks is appropriate for a given grade level. In a reading–writing workshop, the vocabulary in the read-aloud book may exceed the level of most of the children in the class. In a reading–writing workshop, students read texts that are not controlled, limited, and curated for all students in a grade level. Rather, students are directed to texts that are "just right" for their assessed reading levels. Students have more choices in a reading–writing workshop, but many skills in grammar, spelling, and vocabulary often go unaddressed.

Basal reader programs emphasize discreet, sequential skills of reading and writing, which are explicitly laid out in the textbook and workbook. reading–writing workshop teaches reading as a process that involves the simultaneous use of multiple skills, which are explained and modeled by the teacher *as* she reads and writes. The reading–writing workshop teacher decides on the mini-lessons (teaching points), the small group instruction, the features of author's craft to be highlighted during the read-aloud, the activities to be done in the word study center, and the content of the conversations that take place during conference time. The quality of the reading–writing workshop, then, will not be better than the perception, knowledge, and teaching skills of the individual teacher. That is why the reading–writing workshop requires extensive professional development, and that is why, in many cases, it fails to achieve its potential.

Basal readers specify the vocabulary to be taught by giving lists of words drawn from the literature. (Usually, these lists look like a collection of unrelated words, even though they all come from the same story.) The reading–writing workshop offers the opportunity for more durable vocabulary learning *if* the teacher knows how to select and teach useful, related words, and if she knows how to teach true word-learning skills, such as recognizing words with common roots (not just prefixes and suffixes).

Basal reader programs usually come with ready-made tests and quizzes. In a reading–writing workshop, the teacher assesses student progress informally, keeping ongoing records and setting goals with individual students.

Teachers using a basal reader make instructional decisions based mainly on the date: if it's November, then I should be on Unit 4, "Life in the City." Reading–writing workshop teachers make instructional decisions based on how their students are progressing. They monitor progress using a variety of methods: observation and notations, checklists, rubrics, anecdotal records, homemade and standardized tests.

Vocabulary should be—but generally is not—present in every part of balanced literacy and reading–writing workshop. In every read-aloud, the teacher should stop to briefly define at least one word and should spark an interaction (a few yes/no questions) with at least one other word. In every shared reading, at least two words should be highlighted and explained, not just with a brief definition, but with examples and associations. In every guided reading lesson where the teacher visits groups around the room, at least one word should be focused on in a strategic way. Word study time should rotate vocabulary, spelling, and grammar, but these skills should bleed into each other. Conferences should nurture vocabulary use in reading and writing. As teachers listen to children and help them express themselves, they should recast the children's thoughts with elevated vocabulary.

If this seems like overemphasis on vocabulary, I would ask, *At the expense of what?*

Given the pivotal role of vocabulary in virtually all aspects of academic competence, it is alarming that classroom research consistently reveals how relatively little focused academic vocabulary instruction actually occurs in the typical K–12 classroom. For example, Durkin (1979) found that upper-elementary teachers spent less than 1% of their overall reading instruction focused on vocabulary. More recently, Scott and Nagy (1997) documented the paucity of vocabulary instruction in 23 ethnically diverse upper-elementary classrooms, reporting that only 6% of school time was devoted to vocabulary, with only 1.4% allowed to content area vocabulary. Biemiller (2001) reached a similar conclusion, noting that there appears to be a relatively little explicit vocabulary teaching in the elementary grades. The scarcity of systematic, intentional vocabulary and language teaching has also been documented in programs serving English learners (Dutro and Moran, 2003; Gersten and Baker, 2000; Scarcella, 1996). Duty and Moran (2003) and Filmore and Snow (2000) emphasize that simply exposing second language students to English-language rich, interactive classrooms is woefully insufficient; intensive instruction of academic vocabulary and related grammatical knowledge must be carefully orchestrated across the subject areas for language minority students to attain rigorous content standards.

(Feldman and Kinsella, 2005, 2)

A lot of school-wide work and commitment goes into making reading–writing workshop successful. Not everyone is going to be on board, unfortunately. No one says reading–writing workshop is easier than program-based teaching, but—when it does work well—it is extremely rewarding. If you are new to reading–writing workshop, or struggling with it, you might like to know about the challenges that the literacy coaches have noticed. Barb Golub, a literacy coach and my co-author of *Infusing Grammar into the Writer's Workshop* (Routledge, 2016), points out three points of concern: First, to create independent and engaged readers, teachers need to resist the temptation to simply hand out books to children. The reading–writing workshop philosophy is to allow children to select their own independent reading books from a well-stocked classroom and school library. However, there have to also be some guidance, rules, and limitations to foster actual reading growth. Second, teachers have to remember that reading–writing workshop cannot be the only literacy instruction across the day. The other components of balanced literacy—read aloud, word study, interactive and shared writing, shared reading, and writing workshop—should also be in place in a daily/weekly schedule. In other words, the term *reading–writing workshop* is used loosely, but we have to remember that it is meant to fit into a context of a full, well-thought-out, balanced literacy suite of experiences. Third, sometimes teachers miss the difference between naming a skill and actually teaching that skill. Rather than saying, "Today, I want to teach you to infer," we should say and think of it this way:

> Today, I want to teach you that you need to pay attention to how characters are feeling, even when the author isn't telling you. When you turn each page, study the picture and think, 'How is this character feeling?' Continue reading only when you are sure. If you're not sure, think about what's happening in the book. How would you feel?

That kind of language teaches the metacognitive strategy *that results in* inference-making. We have to do more than telling students to execute a skill. We have to show them what good readers do in their heads. It is the execution of the skill that is assessed, not the naming of the skill.

If we believe in reading–writing workshop, then we need to shore up its weaknesses, one of which is vocabulary. (The other two are grammar and spelling.) Reading–writing workshop is not without its detractors, those who "wish we could just use our basal again." The basals, they argue, come with a foolproof scope and sequence of skills aligned to the readings. But proponents of reading–writing workshop argue that basal reading programs, often scripted, are calendar-driven, not data driven, as the workshop model is. One criticism of the workshop model is that it is not rigorous. Indeed, without well-planned, meaningful, and memorable vocabulary instruction embedded in the reading–writing workshop, the model does lack rigor. Reading alone is *not* enough because reading alone will not teach children about word components, and will simply not work fast enough for children who come to school with deficient background knowledge, let alone children who are learning English, and children with special needs, including hearing impairments.

To understand the relationship between reading–writing workshop and balanced literacy, think of the pop music group Gladys Knight and the Pips. Gladys may get the name recognition, and she certainly deserves it, but there was a reason why she kept her backups. (And, yes, now would be a good time to ask your parents who Gladys Knight is. While you're at it, go listen to "Midnight Train to Georgia." You won't be sorry.)

Conference Time

Conferring is a form of tutoring in which the teacher provides guidance and instruction that is best done one-to-one. (When conference time turns into teaching that could just as well be done in a group, it has missed its opportunity and purpose.)

Dan Reynolds and Amanda Goodwin (2016, 26), in describing how to scaffold complex texts, suggest several questions that teachers can choose from when they see that a child needs individual help with word meanings in a text:

1. Cue for metacognition: Are there hard words you need to figure out?
2. Cue for using strategies: What do you know that can help you figure out some of these?
3. Check for specific word knowledge: What do you think (specific word) means? How do you know?
4. Cue for morphological understandings: Are there parts of this word that you recognize? What do these parts tell you? Let me see you point to the part of the word that you recognize. What does it mean? Now, what do you think the whole word might mean?
5. For troublesome words, provide examples, connect to experiences, provide visuals: OK, this word is *hover*. Rhymes with *cover*. Have you ever seen the way a bumble bee seems to stay still while it's flying over a flower? That's hovering. Flies can't do that, can they? They can't hover. They can't stand still while flying like a bee can.
6. Help the student interpret the context: I see somewhere else in (or near) the sentence that means the same as (specific word). Can you find it?

Archaic Words and Jargon

When students are reading a book set in a very distant time and place, such as *The Midwife's Apprentice* by Karen Cushman, which is set in medieval rural England, they will encounter many words, especially nouns, that name unfamiliar objects and roles of people. The best way to handle these archaic or highly localized words is to provide a glossary that gives student-friendly definitions and visuals. You can even have students create the glossaries as a word wall if this is one of your read-aloud or guided-reading selections. For independent reading, you might provide a student-created (laminated and saved from year to year) glossary, handed to the students along with the book.

In a book like *The Midwife's Apprentice*, we also encounter words whose meanings differ from how we might use them today. For example, today we think of a *bailiff* as a uniformed court officer who oversees order in the courtroom as a kind of assistant to the judge. In *The Midwife's Apprentice*, a bailiff serves a more generalized purpose. Other archaic or highly localized words from *The Midwife's Apprentice* are *apprentice, bodice, bonny, breeches, comfrey, cumin, midwife, moil, mutton, privy, soothsayer, vellum,* and *wimple.*

All fields of knowledge have their jargon. *Johnny Tremain* is another popular book with highly specific vocabulary, the jargon of silversmithing. The reader encounters *anneal, apprentice, trencher, crucible, molten, artisan, boatswain,* and numerous military words.

It is not necessary for students to come away with detailed knowledge of these very specific terms. If we had all the time in the world, we could explore them, but our allotted time for explicit vocabulary instruction is limited and has to be devoted to words for wider use. It is sufficient for students to glean a superficial time-of-need knowledge of archaic nouns, highly localized vocabulary, and jargon.

Bibliography

Benjamin, Amy and Barbara Golub. (2016). *Infusing Grammar into the Writer's Workshop.* New York: Eye on Education. 1–11.

Biemiller, Andrew. (2001). Teaching Vocabulary in the Primary Grades: Vocabulary Instruction Needed. In J.F. Baumann and E.J. Kame'enui (Eds.), *Vocabulary Instruction: From ReSearch to Practice* (pp. 159–176). New York: Guilford Press.

Cushman, Karen. (1995). *The Midwife's Apprentice.* Boston, MA: Houghton Mifflin Harcourt.

Durkin, Delores. 1979. What classroom observations reveal about reading comprehension instruction. *Reading Research Quarterly,* 14, 481–533. Cited in Sejnost, Roberta L. and Sharon M. Thiese. (2010). *Building Content Literacy: Strategies for the Adolescent Learner.* Thousand Oaks, CA: Corwin. 21.

Dutro, A. and C. Moran. (2003). Rethinking English Language Instruction: An Architectural Approach. In G. Garcia (Ed.), *English Learners: Reaching the Highest Level of English Literacy* (pp. 227–258). Newark, DE: International Reading Association.

Feldman, Kevin and Kate Kinsella. (2005). Narrowing the Language Gap: The Case for Explicit Vocabulary Instruction. *Scholastic Professional Paper*. New York: Scholastic Inc. 2.

Fillmore, L.W. and C.E. Snow. (2000). What Teachers Need to Know About Language. Special report from ERIC Clearinghouse on language and linguistics. http://www.cal.org/ericcll/teachers/teachers.pdf.

Gersten, R. and S. Baker. (2000). Effective Instruction for English-Language Learners: What We Know About Effective Insertional Practices for English-Language Learners. *Exceptional Children*, 66(4), 454–470.

Reynolds, Dan and Amanda P. Goodwin. (2016). Making Complex Texts Reality for All Students: Dynamic Scaffolding That Bridges the Gaps Between Student and Text. *Voices from the Middle*, 23(4), 25–31.

Scarcella, R.C. (1996). Secondary Education and Second Language Research: ESL Students in the 1990s. *The CATESOL Journal*, 9, 129–152.

Scott, J.A. and William E. Nagy. (1997). Understanding the Definitions of Unfamiliar Words. *Reading Research Quarterly*, 32, 184–200.

Appendix B
The Coxhead List: The Academic Word List (AWL) and Spanish Cognates, Organized by Frequency

Unlike Tier III words, which are specific to particular fields of study and are appropriate for a textbook glossary, Tier II words are generic, used across subject areas, albeit with shades of meaning that apply to different subjects. With thousands of words in English that could be considered Tier II, which might be the most important, and how would we decide?

The answer to that question was explored in detail by Averil Coxhead, who, in 2000, created what is known in the field of linguistics as the Academic Word List (AWL). The list contains 570 word families (words that can be morphed into other forms by adding prefixes and suffixes) that were selected *because they appear frequently and consistently across a wide range of academic texts.* The list does not include the Tier I words that are in the most frequent 2,000–3,000 words of English (Coxhead, 2006). (Those words are listed in what is called the General Service List, developed originally by Michael West in 1953, and revised several times since.) As many as 10% of the nouns, verbs, adjectives, and adverbs in academic texts appear on the AWL, as opposed to only 1.4% of the words in fictional texts and poetry. What that means is that to make the transition from fiction and poetry to informational and persuasive text, readers need to know a great many more words that are on the AWL.

The AWL is organized into ten subsets, arranged in the order of frequency that the words appear in academic text. The words are arranged alphabetically within each subset. The sooner students learn the words in Subset 1, the more capable they will be as readers of informational text at the elementary level. Subset 1 contains the words that are the most common in academic text, followed by Subset 2, and so on.

Learning the words on the AWL is not a matter of learning definitions. As you look the list over yourself, think about how you learned these words. You probably learned very few of them, if any, by being explicitly taught their meanings or by consulting a dictionary. You learned them by being in school and by participating in conversations that used these words. You learned to broaden and narrow their meanings as a result of repeated exposure in a variety of contexts and forms.

The AWL words should be "caught, not taught," which is to say, you should use them consciously, purposefully, and consistently in your speech, and help students understand them in their readings. By giving students a "concentrated dose" of the words, subset by subset over a period of time throughout the school year, you ensure that these important words become more and more familiar to your students. In addition, you can and should reinforce them through game-playing and puzzle-solving (Chapter 4).

The following words, along with Spanish cognates, where applicable, are a slightly modified version of the Academic Word List (Coxhead, 2000).

Why Include Spanish Cognates?

The word *cognate* itself has a Latin root, meaning *common* (co-) *birth* (*gnasci*). It is related to the word *recognize* and even the word *know*. It is obvious that Spanish cognates are a convenient bridge to English for Spanish speakers. What may be less obvious is that English speakers who don't even know any Spanish (or the other Romance languages: French, Italian, Portuguese, Romanian) can deepen their understanding of Tier II English words just by hearing the Spanish cognates and seeing them in written form. As sound-alikes and look-alikes, these cognates offer one more dimension of exposure and opportunity to process. Learning about cognates improves a student's awareness of structural analysis. As students notice certain word endings in Spanish (*-amente, -edad, -oso*, etc.), they become more aware of the corresponding word endings in English (*-ly, -tude, -ious*, etc.). Strategic awareness of cognates benefits everyone.

According to the U.S. Census Bureau (2012), approximately eight and a half million school-aged children (in the United States) speak Spanish, either primarily or in addition to English. Some 70% of American English language learners are native Spanish speakers, so we're talking about a very significant segment of our school population who can benefit from efforts that help them use their Spanish to access English, especially academic English.

> Many ELLs do not automatically recognize cognates in their second language and need explicit cognate instruction to help them use their Spanish to learn English. On the other hand, even kindergarteners can be taught to use cognates. Any teacher can teach cognates: you do not have to speak Spanish. Dip into the NTC's Dictionary of Spanish Cognates by Rose Nash.
>
> (Borah-Geller, 2010)

For those who are already bilingual in Spanish and English, pointing out cognates makes immediate sense. For those who are conversant only in Spanish, pointing out cognates will help them learn English, especially the Tier II (words of academics and business). And monolingual native speakers of English can also benefit from learning Spanish cognates.

Unsurprisingly, about 90% of the words on the Academic Word List have Spanish cognates (and cognates in other Latin-based languages: French, Italian, Portuguese, Romanian).

Native Spanish speakers will at first and naturally ascribe the meaning of the Spanish word to its English "version." Not all cognates convert to exactly the same meaning in both languages. But that fact in itself can give us insight into the word's meaning in English. For example, the Spanish word *actualmente* means *currently*, not *actually*, as you might think. But when you understand that there is a relationship between *currently* and *actually*, you get a deeper understanding of both words. Here's another example: the Spanish word *decepción* means *disappointment*, not, as you might think, *deception*. But thinking about the poignant relationship between deception and disappointment gives you deep insight into both words in English. Comparison-contrast is a key form of critical thinking.

Words that appear to be cognates but are actually not are like people that you could swear are related because of their similar appearances, but who are actually not. We call such unrelated but look-alike words *false cognates*. Only about 10% of word pairs are false cognates. For example, the Spanish word *carpeta* means *folder*, not *carpet*. The Spanish word *asistir* means to *attend*, not *to assist*. Most Spanish words that look like English words do share a meaning, but sometimes the shared meaning requires that you do some convergent thinking (thinking about similarities in seemingly unlike things).

Knowledge of Spanish and other Latin-based languages is a rich power source for learning the set of words on the AWL. Knowing these words can mean the difference between success and frustration at school. Even if students are exposed to conversational English outside of school, the English words they are exposed to are probably Tier I. Tier I words in English are Germanic-based, for the most part. Germanic-based words are not Spanish cognates, so conversations among friends may not lead to learning academic English words. For example, a child may quickly learn the English words *ball*, or *play ball*, or *play ball with us after school*. That's great, but we don't talk or read about playing ball when learning in the classroom. For classroom learning, though, we do use close to a hundred words that derive from the Spanish verb *tener* (to have)—a word that is definitely in the Spanish-speaking child's vocabulary. But with that simple word—*tener*—a Spanish-speaking child can unlock words used in academic life, including *retain, detain, obtain, attain, maintain, contain, ascertain, certain,* and all of their forms (*retention, detention, attainment, maintenance,* etc.).

Subset 1

analyze, approach, area, assess, assume, authority, available, benefit, concept, consist, context, constitute, contract, data, define, derive, distribute, economy, environment, establish, estimate, evident, factor, finance, formula, function, income, indicate, individual, interpret, involve, issue, labor, legal, legislate, method, occur, percent, period, principle, proceed, process, policy, require, research, respond, role, section, sector, significant, source, specific, structure, theory, vary

Subset 1: Spanish Cognates

analizar, el área, asumir, la autoridad, el beneficio/beneficiar, concepto, consistir, contexto, constituir, datos, definir, derivar, distribuir, la economía, establecer, estimar/estimado, evidente, la función, las finanzas, la fórmula, el índice, el individuo, interpretar, envolver, laborar, legal, legislar, el método, ocurrir, el por ciento, el período, principio, proceder, el proceso, requerir, responder, rol sección, sector, significativo/significante, específico, la estructura, la teoría, variar

Subset 2

achieve, acquire, administrate, affect, appropriate, aspect, assist, category, commission, complex, conduct, consequence, construct, consume, credit, culture, design, distinct, element, evaluate, feature, impact, institute, invest, maintain, obtain, perceive, positive, potential, previous, primary, range, region, regulate, relevant, reside, resource, restrict, secure, select, site, strategy, survey, tradition, transfer

Subset 2: Spanish Cognates

adquirir, administrar, afectar, apropiado, el aspecto, la categoría, la comisión, complejo, conducta, consiguiente, construir, consumir, el crédito, la cultura, diseñar, distinto, el elemento, evaluar, el impacto, instituto, invertir, mantener, obtener, percibir, positivo, potencial, previo, primero, región, regular, relevante, residir, restringir, seguro, selecto, sitio, la estrategia, la tradición, transferir

Subset 3

alternative, circumstance, comment, compensate, consent, considerable, constant, constrain, contribute, convene, coordinate, core, corporate, correspond, criteria, deduce, demonstrate, document, dominate, emphasis, ensure, exclude, framework, fund, illustrate, immigrate, imply, initial, instance, interact, justify, layer, link, maximize, negate, outcome, philosophy, physical, proportion, publish, react, register, rely, scheme, sequence, shift, specify, sufficient, technical, technique, valid, volume

Subset 3: Spanish Cognates

el alternativo, la circunstancia, el comentario, compensar, consentimiento, constante, considerable, contribuir, la coordenada, corporativo, corresponden, los criterios, deducen, demonstrar, el documento, dominan, el énfasis, el fondo, ilustrar, inmigrar, la instancia, inicial, interactuar, justificar, maximiza, la filosofía, la proporción, registrar, especificar, volumen

Subset 4

access, adequacy, annual, apparent, approximate, attitude, attribute, civil, code, commit, concentrate, confer, contrast, cycle, debate, despite, dimension, domestic, emerge, ethnic, grant, hence, hypothesis, implement, implicate, impose, integrate, internal, investigate, mechanism, occupy, option, output, overall, parallel, parameter, phrase, prior, principal, professional, project, promote, regime, resolve, retain, series, statistic, status, stress, subsequent, undertake

Subset 4: Spanish Cognates

acceso, la adecuación, la actitud, aparente, anual, aproximado, atributo, civil, cometer, concentrarse, conferir, el contraste, el ciclo, debatir, la dimensión, étnico, la hipótesis, implementar, imponer, integrar, interno, investigar, el mecanismo, ocupar, la opción, paralelo, el parámetro, la frase, el profesional, el proyecto, promover, resolver, retener, la serie, la estadística, el estrés

Subset 5

academy, adjust, alter, amend, capacity, clause, compound, consult, decline, discrete, enable, energy, enforce, entity, equivalent, evolve, expand, expose, external, facilitate, fundamental, generate, liberal, license, logic, margin, modify, monitor, network, notion, objective, orient, perspective, precise, prime, psychology, pursue, ratio, reject, revenue, stable, style, substitute, sustain, symbol, target, transit, trend, version, welfare, whereas

Subset 5: Spanish Cognates

la academia, ajustar, alterar, enmendar, la capacidad, la clásula, compuesto, consultar, la energía, la entidad, equivalente, evolucionar, exponer, externo, facilitar, fundamental, generar, liberal, la licencia, la lógica, el margen, modificar, el monitor, la noción, el objetivo, orientar, la perspectiva, preciso, principal, la psicología, perseguir, el estable, el estilo, el sustituto, el símbolo, el tránsito, la versión

Subset 6

abstract, accuracy, acknowledge, aggregate, allocate, assign, bond, capable, cite, cooperate, discriminate, display, diverse, domain, edit, enhance, estate, exceed, explicit, federal, fee, flexible, furthermore, gender, incentive, incorporate, incidence, index, inhibit, initiate, input, interval, mitigate, minimum, ministry, motive, neutral, nevertheless, overseas, precede, presume, rational, recover, reveal, scope, subsidy, trace, transform, underlie, utilize

Subset 6: Spanish Cognates

abstracto, el agregado, asignar, capaz, citar, cooperar, discriminar, diverso, el dominio, editar, la estancia, exceder, explícito, federal, flexible, el género, el incentivo, incorpora,r la incidencia, el índice inhibir, iniciar, el intervalo, el mínima, el misisterio, el motivo, neutral, preceder, presumir, racional recuperar, revelar, transformar, utilizar

Subset 7

adapt, advocate, channel, classic, comprehensive, comprise, confirm, contrary, convert, decade, deny, differentiate, dispose, dynamic, equip, eliminate, empirical, extract, finite, foundation, gradient, guarantee, hierarchy, identical, ideology, infer, innovate, insert, intervene, isolate, media, mode, paradigm, phenomenon, priority, prohibit, publication, quote, release, reverse, simulate, sold, somewhat, submit, successor, thesis, transmit, ultimate, unique, voluntary

Subset 7: Spanish Cognates

adaptarse, el canal, clásico, comprehender, confirmar, contrario, convertir, la década, diferenciar, disponer, dinámico, equipar, eliminar, empírico, extraer, finito, la fundación, el gradiente, garantizar, idéntico, la ideología, inferir, insertar, intervenir, los medios de comunicación, el modo/la modalidad, el paradigma, fenómeno, la prioridad, prohibir, la publicación, el revés, simular, el sucesor, la tesis, transmitir, único

Subset 8

abandon, accompany, accumulate, ambiguous, appendix, appreciate, arbitrary, automate, bias, chart, clarify, commodity, complement, conform, contemporary, contradict, crucial, currency, denote, detect, deviate, displace, eventual, exhibit, exploit, fluctuate, guideline, implicit, induce, inevitable, infrastructure, inspect, intense, manipulate, minimize, nuclear, offset, predominant, prospect, radial, reinforce, restore, revise, tension, terminate, theme, thereby, uniform, vehicle, via, virtual, widespread

Subset 8: Spanish Cognates

abandonar, acompañar, acumular, ambiguo, el apéndice, arbitrario, aclara,r el complemento, contemporaneo, contradecir, crucial, denotar, detectar, desplazar, la exposición, explotar, fluctua,r implícito, inducir, inevitable, la infraestructura, inspeccionar, intenso, manipular, minimiza, nuclear, el prospecto, radial, reforzar, revisar, la tensión, terminar, la tema, el uniforme, el vehículo, vía, virtual

Subset 9

accommodate, analogy, anticipate, assure, attain, behalf, cease, coherent, coincide, commence, compatible, concurrent, confine, controversy, converse, device, devote, diminish, distort, duration, erode, ethic, format, found, inherent, insight, integral, intermediate, manual, mature, mediate, medium, military, minimal, mutual, norm, overlap, passive, portion, preliminary, protocol, qualitative, refine, restrain, revolution, rigid, route, scenario, sphere, subordinate, supplement, suspend, trigger, unify, violate

Subset 9: Spanish Cognates

analogia, cesar, coherente, coincidir, comenzar, compatible, concurrente, confinar, la controversia, conversar, disminuir, distorsionar, la duración, erosionar, fundar, el formato, inherente, la percepción, integrante, intermedio, manual, mediar, medio, mínimo, mutuo, la norma, pasivo, la porción, preliminar, el protocolo, refinar, la revolusión, rigido, la ruta, el escenario, la esfera, subordinar, el suplemento, suspender, unificar, violar

Subset 10

adjacent, albeit, assemble, collapse, colleague, compile, conceive, convince, depress, encounter, forthcoming, incline, integrity, intrinsic, invoke, levy, likewise, nonetheless, notwithstanding, ongoing, panel, persist, pose, reluctance, so-called, straightforward, undergo, whereby

Subset 10: Spanish Cognates

adyacente, el colapso, el colega, compilar, convencer, el encuentro, inclinarse, la integridad, intrínsic, invocar, el panel, persistir, posar

Bibliography

Borah-Geller, Lisa. (2010). Center for the Collaborative Classroom. *How Can Cognates "Beneficiar" English Langauge Learners?* www.collaborative classroom.org/blog/2010/07/21/how-can-cognates-beneficiar-english-language-learners-ells.

Coxhead, Averil. (2006). *Essentials of Teaching Academic Vocabulary*. 1st Edition. Boston, MA: Heinle. 146–151.

United States Census Bureau. (2012). Census.gov. Accessed November 20, 2016.

Zwier, Lawrence J. (2002). *Building Academic Vocabulary*. Ann Arbor, MI: University of Michigan Press. ix–x.

Appendix C
The Zwier List: Basic Toolkit of Academic Vocabulary, Organized by Purpose

The following list is adapted from Lawrence J. Zwier's *Building Academic Vocabulary*. We've whittled Zwier's list down to the words that we think are the most essential and accessible for elementary and middle school students. Think of it as a mini-version of the Academic Word List (AWL). This list is particularly useful for English language learners. But don't think of it as a vocabulary list in the traditional way of having students learn definitions. Think of the words as cues for you to (1) use in class when talking about subjects such as social studies, science, and math, and (2) provide sentence frames for students to process information they are learning in these subjects.

List 1: Words about Inclusion in a Group or Whole

Verbs: *consist of, be composed of, involve, include, contain, make up, form* (Spanish cognates: *consistir, componer, involucrar, incuir*)

Nouns: *category, range, department, section* (Spanish cognates: *la categoría, el departamento, la sección*)

Adjectives: *partial, entire, complete* (Spanish cognates: *partial, completo*)

Good to know: Adverbs that limit the extent of something often accompany these verbs: *mostly, primarily, largely*. Native speakers know that these adverbs usually wedge themselves between the verb and the preposition *of*. English language learners may need to learn this concept by hearing the pattern repeatedly, having the pattern brought to their attention, and then consciously practicing the pattern in an authentic context (not a worksheet).

Useful for: steps in a process or event; components of a system or group

List 2: Words about Equivalence

Verbs: *equal, agree* (Spanish cognates: *igual*)

Nouns: *equality, similarity, agreement* (Spanish cognates: *la igualidad*)

Adjectives: *equivalent, alike, identical, typical, similar* (Spanish cognates: *equivalente, idéntico, típico*)

Good to know: English language learners, particularly, will probably have trouble knowing how to use the various prepositions that generally follow these words: *to, in, of, between*. Getting the hang of this is more a matter of hearing repeated use (perceiving a pattern that comes to "sound right") rather than explaining the abstract concepts behind them. A third grader is not going to understand or be able to apply an explanation such as, "We say similar *in* when we're talking about particular features. We say similar *to* when we're talking comparing two wholes to each other." But she will be able to pick up the patterns if they are deliberately repeated.

List 3: Words about Differences

Verbs: *differ, disagree* (Spanish cognates: *diferir*)
Nouns: *inequality, contrast, difference, gap, disagreement* (Spanish cognates: *la desigualdad, el contraste, la diferencia*)
Adjectives: *unequal, different* (Spanish cognates: *diferente*)
Good to know: Notice the quirky difference in the prefixes between *inequality* and *unequal*.

List 4: Lists about Changes

Verbs: *increase, decrease, alter, modify, translate, convert, raise, lower, accelerate, expand, reduce, contract, decline, transform* (Spanish cognates: *alter, modifier, converter, acelerar, reducer, transformar*)
Nouns: *increase, decrease, alteration, translation, conversion, acceleration, expansion reduction, contraction, decline* (Spanish cognates: *la modificación, la traducción, la conversión, la expansión, la reducción*)
Good to know: All of the verbs about change are transitive verbs. That is, they require a direct object, something that is being changed. Therefore, there are always three elements in a sentence about change: the change agent (the subject), the verb (indicating the kind of change), and the object that is being changed. This three-part formula for a sentence about change is a convenient sentence frame that will help students think about and express their knowledge about changes. Much of the thinking we do in science relates to the topic of changes.

List 5: Words about Links

Verbs: *link, connect, blend* (Spanish cognates: *conectar*)
Nouns: *link, connection, blend* (Spanish cognates: *la conexión*)
Good to know: English language learners may need help knowing that we say *link to; connect to* or *connect with; blend with* or *blend in with*.

List 6: Words about Causes and Effects

Verbs: *stem from, be due to, lead to, yield, generate, promote, be responsible for, affect* (Spanish cognates: *general, promocionar, responsable, afectar*)

Nouns: *effect, result* (Spanish cognates: *el efecto, el resultado*)

Good to know: *Affect* and *effect* are confusing, even for educated people! Although both *affect* and *effect* can each be used as both a verb or a noun, *affect* is usually a verb; *effect*, usually a noun. If you associate the phrase *the effect(s)* (exaggerating the *e* sound), that may help.

List 7: Words about Facilitation

Verbs: *clear the way for, remove obstacles to, permit, allow, ease, pave the way for, approve* (Spanish cognates: *permitir, pavimentar*)

Nouns: *permission, approval* (Spanish cognates: *el permiso, la aprobación*)

Good to know: You will find these words and phrases frequently in social studies text.

List 8: Words about Prevention

Verbs: *prevent, block, cease, restrict, forbid, deny, refuse* (Spanish cognates: *preventir, cesar, restringir*)

Nouns: *obstacle, blockage, denial, refusal, hindrance* (Spanish cognates: *el obstáculo, la obstrucción*)

Good to know: That verbs dominate this list is not a coincidence. Verbs are powerful. When we choose the right verb, the rest of the sentence snaps into place, eliminating wordiness.

Bibliography

Zwier, Lawrence J. (2002). *Building Academic Vocabulary*. Ann Arbor, MI: University of Michigan Press. ix–x.

Appendix D
Analysis of Forty Latin and Greek Word Roots for Mini-Lessons

The time you spend in teaching Latin word roots as mini-lessons will pay off in myriad ways. Learning any of the following roots will yield knowledge of several related words, and then each related word that has developed from a given root will be made more memorable because the words are connected by a common meaning. Because of their connectedness, these words often appear together in the same text, so learning them together can strengthen comprehension in a reading piece and build cohesion in a writing piece. The study of etymology not only illuminates meaning; it also enlightens us about the social and cultural nature of language itself. We know that words have shades of meaning in various contexts, with some words being variable and others more fixed. But word meanings can also vary over time, sometimes to the extent that etymologists puzzle over their origins. Like family members who move far away from their relatives, some words, over time, are used in ways that resemble their relatives on the etymology tree only vaguely, leaving us to wonder. And, let's not forget that knowledge about Latin and Greek roots makes us less intimidated by long words, giving us a tool for breaking them down.

The trouble is, lists of word roots alone are not engaging, and therefore not memorable. We need to create activities for students to engage them in each word root. One such way can be in the form of a mini-lesson, as follows:

How to structure the mini-lesson (note that this mini-lesson can be broken up over several days):

1. Draw a tree. As "apples" on the tree, write a few examples of familiar words sharing the same root.
2. Using think-pair-share, ask students to talk about what the (familiar) words mean. Then, ask them to make a hypothesis as to what all of these words have in common.
3. Write the root and its brief definition on the base of the tree.
4. Add two or three more words to the tree. Use the list that follows as a source for appropriate words.
5. Use each new word in several sentences that have enough context to reveal their meaning. Don't hesitate to change the form of the word in your sentences.

6. Use think-pair-share for each word, asking students to propose a tentative definition.
7. Verify the definition, using an age-appropriate dictionary. The dictionary feature on Vocabulary.com provides definitions, examples, and personal connections in student-friendly language.
8. Complete the tree diagram by adding the new words and brief definitions.

1. Latin word: *cadere*
   Means: to fall
   Inside the words, it takes these forms: *cad-, cas-, cat-, cid-*
   Examples: *accident, incident/incidental/incidentally, coincide/coincidence, category/categorize, catalogue, decadent/decadence, catapult, deciduous, cataract, cascade, catastrophe/catastrophic*

Later in their schooling, students will encounter more sophisticated words, such as *casualty*, *recidivism*, *cadence*, and *cadenza*.

Spanish cognates: *caer* (to fall); *accidente* (accident), *incidente* (incident), *categoría* (category), *la catapulta* (catapult, noun), *catapultar* (catapult, verb)

Teachable moments: It's easy enough to see the connection between *accident* and *falling*, but the word *accident* originally just meant *a happening*, as today we would use the word *incident*. It might be fun to have students explain the difference between an accident and an incident. They might see that when we use the word *incident*, we are rarely referring to something good. Students are probably more familiar with the noun *coincidence* than the verb from which it is formed, *coincide*.

We often speak of items that "fall under a category." This collocation ("go-together") reflects the etymology. The word *catalogue* is connected to other *-logue* words, including *dialogue*, *monologue*, and *travelogue*. *Logue* is the Greek root, roughly translated as *discourse*, or, more simply, *communication*. (The word *discourse* is seldom used in K–8 education, and probably not very much in high school either, as it is too formal and structured to describe the type of communication that we do with children and young teenagers.) The word *catalogue* gets its name from the fact that, in a catalogue, items were traditionally presented in list form, thus "falling."

The word *decadent*, often used to refer to self-indulgence in a pleasure such as chocolate, is related to the word *decay*, which is what your teeth might do if you eat too decadently.

Catapult is ironic. Although a catapult (or the verb, *to catapult*) refers to throwing a spear-like object up into the air, what goes up must come down, hence *catapult* means *that which is driven* (Latin root: *pellere*: *to drive*) *down*.

Cataract and *cascade* can be used to talk about the downward flow of water. Although a cataract is a waterfall, some children may associate it with the ophthalmic condition that their grandparents have, but a cataract of the eye is called so because having one is akin to having your vision blurred by a waterfall.

2. Latin word: *capere*
    Means: to seize, to control
    Inside the words, it takes these forms: *cap-, capt-, -ceive, -cept, cip-*
    Examples: *capture, captain, captive, capacity, anticipate, conceive/concept/
       conception, receive/reception/receipt, deceive/deception/deceit, perceive/
       perception, principle, principal, intercept/interception*

Later in their schooling, students will encounter more sophisticated words, such as *captivate, incipient, inception,* and *precept*.

Spanish cognates: *capitán* (captain), *capacidad* (capacity), *anticiparse*
    (anticipate), *concebir/concepto/concepción* (conceive, concept,
    conception), *recibir/recepto/recepción* (receive, receipt, reception),
    percibir/percepción (perceive, perception), *principio* (principle),
    interceptar/intercepción (intercept, interception)

Teachable moments: We have a spelling-learning opportunity here, did you notice? Three words deriving from this root perfectly follow the *except after C part* of the *i before e* rule. Notice that the verbs *receive, perceive, deceive,* and *conceive* share the same pattern when they convert to nouns: *reception, perception, deception, conception.* And then we have the mysterious silent *p* that shows up in *receipt* but not *deceit. Conception* keeps true to the pronunciation of *concept.*

This is a one-word family whose members scattered far and wide. It may be a little difficult for students to encapsulate (another distant relative) the family resemblances here, but it's worth the conversation, as finding connections among seemingly disparate things strengthens those critical thinking muscles.

3. Latin word: *claudere*
    Means: to close
    Inside the words, it takes these forms: *clos-, claus-, clu-*

Examples: *close, closet, enclose/enclosure, conclude/conclusion/conclusive, clause, claustrophobic, include/inclusive/inclusion, exclude/exclusive/exclusion, seclude/seclusion*

Later in their school, students will encounter more sophisticated words, such as *cloister, recluse/reclusive, occlude/occlusion.*

Spanish cognates: *concluir* (conclude), *incluir* (include), *excluir* (exclude)

Teachable moments: Engage students in a conversation about stories having characters who are recluses. Usually, the recluse in literature has a backstory that explains his solitary habits, and often that backstory holds an important key to the story's plot and themes as a whole. In how many stories does the recluse, someone misunderstood as a pariah or curmudgeon, turn out to save the day?

Everyone understands what it feels like to be claustrophobic. Although *claustrophobia* is a mouthful, it is actually a word that most children learn easily, probably because they can relate so easily to its meaning. Your fourth graders probably know other *-phobia* words: *arachnophobia, hydrophobia, homophobia, xenophobia,* and so on. (For a dizzying list of every kind of phobia imaginable, don't be afraid to check out www.phobialist.com.)

When you are teaching grammar, it might help students understand the concept of a *clause* if they see the relationship between the words *clause* and *conclusion*: you start a thought with a subject, then close it with a predicate, voila—a clause!

4. Latin word: *cognoscere*
    Means: to know, to learn
    Inside the words, it takes these forms: *cogn-, conn-, kno-*
    Examples: *recognize, cognate, knowledge, acknowledge, acquaint*

Later in their school, students will encounter more sophisticated words, such as *cognoscenti, cognition, cognitive, agnostic, cognizant, incognito, reconnaissance, connoisseur.*

Spanish cognates: *reconocer* (recognize)

Teachable moments: My favorite thing about this etymology is that it explains why the word *know*, along with its derivatives, is spelled with that mysterious silent *k*. Phonetically, the hard *g*, hard *c*, and even the *q* are *k* are related (the *g* being the voiced *k*), and so, over time, they branch out, orthographically.

Here's where we can bring in the word *cognate* itself: a cognate simply is a word that we already *know*, or *recognize* from one language to another.

5. Latin word: *credere*
    Means: to believe
    Inside the words, it takes these forms: *cred-*
    Examples: *credit, credible, incredible, credulous, incredulous, discredit*

Later in their school, students will encounter more sophisticated words, such as *credibility, creed, miscreant, accredit, credential.*

Spanish cognates: *crédito* (credit), *creencia* (belief)

Teachable moments: Use this opportunity to teach the difference between *incredible* and *incredulous*. These words are often used as synonyms, incorrectly. Something that is hard to believe is said to be *incredible*. The person who finds it hard to believe is said to be *incredulous*.

Help students understand how the phrase *credit card* gets its name.

6. Latin word: *currere*
    Means: to run
    Inside the words, it takes these forms: *cur-, curs-, cor-*
    Examples: *corridor, current, cursor, cursive, course, occur/occurrence, recur/recurrent, concur/concurrent, excursion*

Later in their schooling, students will encounter more sophisticated words, such as *incorrigible, incursion, cursory,* and *discourse.*

Spanish cognates: *correr* (to run), *carrera* (career), *al corredor* (the corridor), *a la corriente* (the current), *el cursor* (the cursor), *cursivo* (cursive), *el curso* (the course), *ocurrir* (to occur), *recurrir* (to recur), *concurrir* (to concur), *la excursión* (the excursion)

Teachable moments: Although we scold children for running in the halls, they do so anyway. Maybe that's because the word *corridor* derives from the root for *to run.*

Currents run, either in time, in water, in air, or on your computer screen. A course has a beginning and an end: it runs through time.

Cursive writing is called so because the letters run together in a word.

When we say that something is running, we sometimes mean that it is "going on," as in the words *occur* and *recur.* We put the root *cur-* together with the prefix *con-* (with) to create *concur*, meaning agree, or *run together with.*

7. Latin word: *dictare*
   Means: to say
   Inside the words, it takes these forms: *dic-, dict-*
   Examples: *dictate, dictator, dictionary, diction, predict, indicate*

Later in their schooling, students will encounter more sophisticated words, such as *indict, indictment, benediction, malediction, vindicate, edict.*

Spanish cognates: *decir* (to say)

Teachable moments: Here's an instance where a derivative of a word, *dictator*, departs from the word from which it derives, *dictate*. Although a *dictator* does indeed *dictate*, the connotation and meaning of *dictator* takes on a different meaning in degree.

In Spanish, the word *decir* simply means *to say*, but as you can see from the examples, words in English derived from this root tend toward more formal expressions, often legalistic (edict, indict) and religious (benediction).

8. Latin word: *ducere*
   Means: to lead, to guide
   Inside the words, it takes these forms: *duc-, duct-*
   Examples: *produce/production, reduce/reduction, conduct/conduction, deduct/deduction, educate/education, induct/induction, introduce/ introduction, aqueduct, duct*

Later in their schooling, students will encounter more sophisticated words, such as *induce/induction, seduce/seduction, deductive, inductive, conducive*, and *conduit*. In biology, they will learn about bile ducts, tear ducts, hepatic ducts, and lymphatic ducts.

Spanish cognates: *producir* (to produce), *la producción* (the production), *reducir* (to reduce), *la reducción* (the reduction), *la conducta* (the conduct), *conducir* (to conduct), *la conducción* (the driving), *educar* (to educate), *la educación* (the education), *inducción* (the induction), *introducir* (to introduce), *la introducción* (the introduction), *el acueducto* (the aqueduct)

Teachable moments: This root combines many of our common prefixes: *pro-* (forward), *re-* (back, again), *con-* (with), *de-* (down, away from), *e-* (out), *in-* (into) and *intra/o-* (between). It's eye-opening to consider that the word education derives from the word components that mean *to lead or guide out*. *Aqueduct*, of course, is related to water (the color aqua, aquarium, aquatic). And a *duct* is a tube, canal, or pipe whose purpose is to allow the flow of liquid, air, or electricity.

9. Latin word: *esse*
    Means: to exist, to belong, to pertain to
    Inside the words, it takes these forms: *ess-, -sent, -sence, sta-*
    Examples: *essence, essential, absent, present, represent, state, estate, statue*

Later in their schooling, students will encounter more sophisticated words, such as statute, statutory, existential, status

Spanish cognates: *estar* (to be), *estato* (state)

Teachable moments: The word *state* has multiple meanings (to declare; a condition or situation; a unit of government within a country), but all of these variants connect to the recognition of some kind of entity, some kind of entrance into agreed-upon reality. It's an abstract concept that has to do with setting up boundaries and divisions.

10. Latin word: *facere*
    Means: to create
    Inside the words, it takes these forms: *fac-, fact-, fic-, fict-, fab-*
    Examples: *factory, manufacture, fiction, factor, fabric, facility*

Later in their schooling, students will encounter more sophisticated words, such as *facsimile, benefactor, artifact, fabricate, faculty.*

Spanish cognates: *factor* (to factor), *la fábrica* (the fabric), *fabricar* (to manufacture)

Teachable moments: Connect the words *factory* and *manufacture*. Ironically, the etymology of *manufacture* points to the creating of things by hand (*manu-*, as in manual labor and manuscript).

11. Latin word: *ferre*
    Means: to carry; to bear, to bring
    Inside the words, it takes these forms: *fer-*
    Examples: *ferry, prefer, refer, confer, fertile/fertility, fertilize, offer, transfer, differ/different/difference/differentiate, circumference, suffer*

Later in their schooling, students will encounter more sophisticated words, such as *infer, defer, conifer, proliferate, vociferous, aquifer.*

> Spanish cognates: *preferir* (prefer), *diferir* (differ), *referirse* (refer), *transfirir* (transfer), *sufrir* (suffer)

Teachable moments: Some of the derivatives, most notably *suffer*, have wandered afar from their original meanings. But the etymology of *suffer* (using the prefix *su-* as a shortened form of the suffix *sub-*, meaning *under*) refers to endurance while carrying a weight of some kind.

Your students may be interested to know that the name Christopher derives from this root, thus making Christopher the carrier, bearer, or bringer of Christ.

> 12. Latin word: *fluere*
>   Means: to flow
>   Inside the words, it takes these forms: *flu-*
>   Examples: *flush, fluid, fluent, flue, influenza, influence*

Later in their schooling, students will encounter more sophisticated words, such as *flux, fluctuate, confluence, effluvium,* and *affluent.*

> Spanish cognates: *fluir* (to flow), *el fluido* (the fluid), *con fluidez* (fluently), *la influenza* (the flu; i.e., influenza), *la influencia* (the influence)

Teachable moments: Although words emanating from the root *flu-* usually have something to do with the flow of liquid (*flush, fluid*), they sometimes have to do with the flow of air (*flue*), words (*fluent*), ideas and behaviors (*influence*), or even germs (*influenza*).

> 13. Latin word: *frangere*
>   Means: to break
>   Inside the words, it takes these forms: *frag-, frac-, fra-*
>   Examples: *fragile, fragment, fracture, frail, fray, infraction*

Later in their schooling, students will encounter more sophisticated words, such as *refract, fractal, frangible, fracture.*

> Spanish cognates: *fracción* (fraction), *fragmento* (fragment), *frágil* (fragile), *fractura* (fracture)

Teachable moments: Combine this with a lesson in environmental science: the controversial drilling technology known as *fracking* gets its name from this Latin root. In fracking, shale rock within the earth is blasted open to allow access to natural gas trapped inside the rocks.

You might want to set up an array of adjectives on the concept of flexibility: on one extreme, we have *brittle, inflexible, rigid*. On the other, *flexible, malleable, pliable, elastic*.

14. Latin word: *gradum*
    Means: step
    Inside the words, it takes these forms: *grad-, gress-, gree-*
    Examples: *grade, agree, graduate, progress, gradual, degrade, gradient, biodegradable, aggressive, degree*

Later in their schooling, students will encounter more sophisticated words, such as *digress/digression, transgress/transgression, regress/regression/regressive*.

Spanish cognates: *el grado* (the grade), *graduarse* (to graduate), *el graduado* (the male graduate), *la graduada* (the female graduate), *el egresado* (the male graduate), *la egresada* (the female graduate), *el progreso* (the progress), *gradual* (gradual), *gradualmente* (gradually), *degradar* (to degrade), *el gradiente* (the grade), *biodegradable* (biodegradable), *agresivo* (aggressive)

Teachable moments: Students use the word *grade* all the time, without thinking of the other words having to do with "to step" that are related to it. We can see how second grade is a step up from first grade, but what about report card grades and a grade on a paper? It has to do with degrees, which is a member of this family.

15. Latin word: *iacere*
    Means: to throw
    Inside the words, it takes these forms: *ject-, jet-*
    Examples: *jet, inject/injection, eject/ejector, reject/rejection, subject, object, project, projectile, adjective*

Later in their schooling, students will encounter more sophisticated words, such as *trajectory, conjecture, objective, subjective, jettison*.

Spanish cognates: *inyectar* (to inject), *la inyección* (the injection), *el objeto* (the object), *el proyecto* (the project), *el proyectil* (the projectile), *el adjetivo* (the adjective)

Teachable moments: Think about adjectives. They are words that are "thrown at" the nouns that they modify. The words *subject* and *object* are not so easy to connect to their etymology. A subject is that which is "thrown under" a larger heading. The prefix *ob-* means *against*, as in *obstacle* and *obstruct*. So the noun *object* has wandered away somewhat from its original meaning, but the verb *object* remains closer to its origins. We find the same with the noun *project* and the verb *project*, which clearly retains its etymological sense of "to throw forward."

16. Latin word: *legere*
    Means: to collect, gather, or read
    Inside the words, it takes these forms: *lect-, leg-*
    Examples: *collect, elect, intellect, neglect, select, dialect, lecture, legend, legible*

Later in their schooling, students will encounter more sophisticated words, such as *lectern, deselect, preselect, dialectical*

Spanish cognates: *electo* (elect), *intelecto* (intellect), *negligencia* (neglect), *selecctionar* (select), *leyenda* (legend), leer (to read)

Teachable moments: The word *legal* and its derivatives (*legislature*, etc.) looks like it might emanate from this root, but etymologists tell us that, more likely, it belongs to the root *lex*, referring to law. In any case, the meanings of words about gathering, collecting, reading, and following a set of rules are all entangled. Laws, after all, can be said to be collections of written rules.

17. Latin word: *liberare*
    Means: to set free
    Inside the words, it takes these forms: *libr-, lib-*
    Examples: *liberate, liberal, library, deliberate, deliver, liberty*

Spanish cognates: *libro* (book)

Teachable moments: Etymologically, to deliver something is both to set it free from your possession, and to set yourself free from it. And, isn't it nice to connect the Spanish word for book, *libro*, with the idea of freedom?

18. Latin word: *ludere*
    Means: to play

Inside the words, it takes these forms: *lud-*
Examples: *delude/delusion, illusion, ludicrous*

Later in their schooling, students will encounter more sophisticated words, such as *interlude, elude/elusive, prelude, allude/allusion.*

Spanish cognates: *eludir* (elude), *aludir* (allude)

Teachable moments: The word *collude* (collusion) has a negative connotation, evoking a conspiracy. It emanates from the notion of "playing together," but doing so sneakily, with impure intent. Allusions play on our imagination, inviting us to think of two works of literature simultaneously. The sense of delight we feel when we pick up on an allusion explains its connection to the root for "play."

19. Latin word: *mittere*
    Means: to send
    Inside the words, it takes these forms: *mit-, miss-*
    Examples: *dismiss/dismissal, admit/admission, permit/permission,*
        commit/commission/committee, transmit/transmission, submit/
        submission, mission, omit/omission

Later in their schooling, students will encounter more sophisticated words, such as: *missionary, emit, emission,* and *remit/remittance.*

Spanish cognates: *admitir* (to admit), *admisión* (the admission), *el permiso* (the permission), *permitir* (to permit), *cometer* (to commit), *transmitir* (to transmit), *la transmisión* (the transmission), *la sumisión* (the submission), *la misión* (the mission), *el misionero* (the male missionary), *la misionara* (the female missionary), *omitir* (to omit), *la omisión* (the omission)

Teachable moments: Except for the word *dismiss*, the other verbs follow the pattern of the verb using *mit-* and the noun shifting to *miss-*. There's an interesting connection of meaning between *admit/admission* when it refers to using a ticket to gain access, as opposed to when it refers to making a confession. Although used in different circumstances, both instances have to do with sending forward (*ad-*). Could it be that the act of admitting to a transgression sends us forward?

20. Latin word: *monere*
    Means: to watch, to warn, to advise, to remember
    Inside the words, it takes these forms: *mon-*

Examples: *demonstrate, monitor, monument, summon*

Later in their schooling, students will encounter more sophisticated words, such as *admonish/admonition, premonition.*

Spanish cognates: *demostrar* (demonstrate), *monumento* (monument)

Teachable moments: When we speak of something as being monumentally important, we mean that it will remembered for a long time. A monitor may be someone who watches us, but a monitor is also something that we watch. Etymologists wonder about the word *money,* which appears to come from this root, but the connection is unclear. We know that the Romans chose mint coins close to the temple of the goddess Juno, whose sacred geese, it is said, gave warning to the Roman military of the invading Gauls.

21. Latin word: *nominare*
    Means: to name
    Inside the words, it takes these forms: *nom-, nym-, non-*
    Examples: *nominate, synonym, antonym, anonymous, eponym, nominal, denominator, pseudonym, monomial, binomial, polynomial*

Spanish cognates: *el nombre* (the name), *nombrar* (to name), *el sinónimo* (the synonym), *el antónimo* (the antonym), *nominal* (nominal), *el denominador* (denominator), *el monomial* (the monomial), *el polinomio* (the polynomial)

Teachable moments: Here we have those odd y's seemingly in the middle of nowhere! They look like a random (and maddening) quirk of spelling, but what those y's in the middle of syllables signify is that they are of Greek origin and they want you to know it. Just like the spelling of our names, especially our last names, bespeaks our family's ancestral heritage, many words of Greek origin do the same thing, and the y's are a telltale sign. You may think this is trivial information, but anything that helps us make associations and patterns, and anything that takes the arbitrariness out of word-learning helps us learn and remember. Any time you can give a reason for something that seemingly has no reason behind it, do it. Note that the Spanish language does not use y's like this. Another reason to point it out.

22. Latin word: *pellere*
    Means: to drive forward
    Inside the words, it takes these forms: *pel-, pul-, puls-, peal-*

Examples: *pulse, propel/propeller, repel/repulsive, impel/impulse/ impulsive, expel, appeal, repeal, catapult*

Later in their schooling, students will encounter more sophisticated words, such as: *compel/compulsive, propulsion, expulsion, pulsate,* and *dispel.*

> Spanish cognates: *el pulso* (the pulse), *pulsar* (to pulse), *la pulsación* (the pulsation), *propulsar* (to propel), *repeler* (to repel), *repulsivo* (repulsive), *impulsar* (to boost, i.e., to provide an impulse), *impeler* (to impel), *expulsar* (to expel), *la apelación* (the appellation, i.e., name), *la catapulta* (the catapult), *catapultar* (to catapult)

Teachable moments: Call attention to the pattern that *pel-* in the verb forms converts to *-pulsion* in the noun forms. Explain the biological function of a pulse, as the sign that blood is being driven through the body, delivering life-sustaining oxygen to the cells. *Catapult* is listed also under the root *cata-*.

23. Latin word: *pendere*
    Means: to hang, to weigh, to pay
    Inside the words, it takes these forms: *pen-, pend-, pond-*
    Examples: *spend, expend/expensive, depend/dependent/dependable, independent/independence, pendant, pendulum, ponder, suspend/ suspension, pending*

Later in their education, students will encounter more sophisticated words, such as *appendage, preponderance, compensate/compensation, impending, expendable, pendulous.*

> Spanish cognates: *depender* (to depend), *dependiente* (dependent), *independiente* (indepndent), *la independencia* (the independence), *el péndulo* (the pendulum), *suspender* (to suspend), *la suspensión* (the suspension)

Teachable moments: We have science connections here, so use visuals to show how the concepts of hanging, weighing, and paying are related. *Ponder* is the outlier; help students understand that to ponder something is to have it weigh heavily in your mind. And when something is pending, it is metaphorically hanging in the air.

24. Latin word: *plicare*
    Means: to fold or wind up

Inside the words, it takes these forms: *plic-, plex-, ply-, pli-*
Examples: *complicate/complex, duplicate, reply, pliable, comply,
   compliant/compliance*

Later in their schooling, students will encounter more sophisticated words,
such as *accomplice, implicit, explicit,* and *explicate.*

Spanish cognates: *complicar* (to complicate), *complejo* (complex), *duplicar*
   (to duplicate), *el duplicado* (the duplicate), *responder* (to respond),
   complaciente (accommodating)

Teachable moments: Students who have taken ballet class will know the
French word *plie,* the bending outward of the knees. The words *apply* and *application* are also in this family, although they have wandered off in meaning
somewhat.

   25. Latin word: *ponere*
       Means: to put or set down
       Inside the words, it takes these forms: *pos-*
       Examples: *pose, position, posture, preposition, expose/exposure, impose/
          imposition, suppose/supposedly, compose/composition, positive/
          positively, propose/proposal, deposit*

Later in their schooling, students will encounter more sophisticated words,
such as *imposition, dispositive, exponent, depose/deposition* and *posit.*

Spanish cognates: *la pose* (the pose), *la postura* (the posture), *la posición*
   (the position), *la preposición* (the preposition), *exponer* (to expose),
   la exposición (the exposition), *imponer* (to impose), *la imposición* (the
   imposition), *suponer* (to suppose), *supuestamente* (the supposition),
   positivo (positive), *proponer* (to propose), *la propuesta* (the proposal),
   depositar (to deposit), *el depósito* (the deposit), *poner* (to put or place)

Teachable moments: A preposition gets its name because it is a word that
is *placed before* (*pre-*) a noun or pronoun that is its object. In this family, we
see a familiar set of prefixes, but notice the difference in the way they are
usually suffixed.

   26. Latin word: *portare*
       Means: to carry
       Inside the words, it takes these forms: *port-*

Examples: *portable, porter, import, export, opportunity, important, portal, port, airport, carport, deport, report, support, transport/transportation*

Later in their schooling, students will encounter more sophisticated words, such as: *portfolio, deportment,* and *purport.*

Spanish cognates: *portátil* (the notebook), *el portero* (the goalkeeper), *importar* (to import), *la importación* (the import), *el importado* (the imported item), *exportar* (to export), *la exportación* (the exportation), *el exportador* (the male exporter), *la oportunidad* (the opportunity), *importante* (important), *el portal* (the portal, i.e., door), *el puerto* (the port), *Puerto Rico* (Puerto Rico, i.e., rich port), *el aeropuerto* (the airport), *deportar* (to deport), *el reporte* (the report), *el transporte* (the transport, i.e., the vehicle that transports), *transportar* (to transport)

Teachable moments: The root *port-* is defined as carry, but it also means passage, which explains the words relating to doors (portal, porch) and ports. "Opportunity knocks but once at any man's door." This saying reaches back into etymology: the word opportunity, broken down, means *against* (*op-*) the door (*port-*).

27. Latin word: *ruptura*
    Means: to break or fracture
    Inside the words, it takes these forms: *rupt-,*
    Examples: *interrupt, erupt, disrupt, abrupt, rupture*

Later in their schooling, students will encounter more sophisticated words, such as *corrupt, rupture,* and *bankrupt.*

Spanish cognates: *interrumpir* (to interrupt), *la erupción* (the eruption), *abrupto* (abrupt), *la ruptura* (the rupture)

Teachable moments: This root is not as productive as some of the others, but the etymology is straightforward, so it makes for a good example of how Latin word roots work.

28. Latin word: *scribere*
    Means: to write
    Inside the words, it takes these forms: *scri-, scrib-, scrip-*
    Examples: *script, scribble, describe, manuscript, Scripture, subscribe/subscription, prescribe/prescription*

Later in their schooling, students will encounter more sophisticated words, such as *inscribe/inscription, transcribe/transcription, circumscribe, proscribe.*

Spanish cognates: *escribir* (to write), *describir* (to describe), *el manuscrito* (the manuscript)

Teachable moments: Notice the spelling pattern, where the *b* in the verbs *describe, prescribe, subscribe* becomes *p* in the noun forms *description, prescription, subscription.* This may seem arbitrary, until we realize that *b* and *p* are what linguists call "minimal pairs," which means that your vocal apparatus is doing the same thing for both sounds, except that the *b* is voiced while the *p* is unvoiced. Other minimal pairs are *v* and *f; d* and *t.* Your English language learners may need this information. Your native speakers may find the relationships among sounds and letters interesting, and it may be one more step toward making sense out of English spelling.

29. Latin word: *seguire*
    Means: to follow
    Inside the words, it takes these forms: *sec-, seque-, sue-*
    Examples: *second, secondary, consecutive, consequence, sequence, pursue*

Later in their schooling, students will encounter more sophisticated words, such as *consequential, inconsequential, subsequent, segue, prosecute, persecute,* and *ensue.*

Spanish cognates: *segundo* (second), *consecutivo* (consecutive), *sequencia* (sequence)

Teachable moments: This etymology explains the mystery behind the word *second.* Unlike *third, fourth, fifth,* and so on, *second* takes its name from the Latin (actually, Indo-European) rather than the ordinal numbers, which descend from Old English (Germanic). This revelation may pique interest in the word *first,* which derives from Old English (Germanic) and is related to form (*forma*) and *-fore.*

30. Latin word: *scandere*
    Means: to climb
    Inside the words, it takes these forms: *scend-, scal-*
    Examples: *ascend, descend, scale, transcend, escalate*

Later in their schooling, students will encounter more sophisticated words, such as *crescendo, condescend.*

Spanish cognates: *ascender* (ascend), *descender* (descend), *trascender* (transcend), *escala* (scale)

Teachable moments: The world-famous opera house in Milan, Italy, is called La Scala. Look at a picture of the inside of it to understand how it got its name. The Italian word for ladder is *scala.*

The word *scale* in English has two entirely different meanings. When we speak of the scales on a fish, we are drawing from the older Germanic meaning related to *skin* and *shell.* When we speak of drawing something to *scale,* or *scaling* a mountain, we are using the word in its more recent Latin-based form. Briefly explaining these differences makes the world of language less chaotic to students.

31. Latin word: *sedere*
    Means: to sit, to settle
    Inside the words, it takes these forms: *sid-, sed-, sess-*
    Examples: *reside/residence/residential, president/preside, sediment, possess, obsess, session*

Later in their schooling, students will encounter more sophisticated words, such as *sedentary, assiduous.*

Spanish cognates: *residir* (reside), *presidente* (president), *sedimento* (sediment), *poseer* (possess), *sesión* (session)

Teachable moments: The word *side* is a false cognate, related to German and not Latin/Greek. But this might be a teachable moment for the many compound words in English that end in *side*: *poolside, alongside, seaside, countryside, fireside, ringside, roadside, upside,* and so on.

32. Latin word: *servare*
    Means: to serve, to keep watch over
    Inside the words, it takes these forms: *serv-*
    Examples: *serve, servant, reserve/reservation, deserve, preserve/preservation, conserve/conservation*

Later in their schooling, students will encounter more sophisticated words, such as *servitude.*

Spanish cognates: *reserva* (reserve), *preservar* (preserve), *conservar* (conserve)

Teachable moments: This root is not to be confused (spelling-wise or meaning-wise) with the word *survive* and its derivatives (*survival, survivor*) or *survey*. In those words, the prefix is actually *sur-*, meaning *under*, which combines with the roots *-viv-* and *-vey*, respectively.

33. Latin word: *specere*
    Means: to see
    Inside the words, it takes these forms: *spec-, spect-, spic-*
    Examples: *spectator, spectacular, inspect, respect, suspect, spectacles*

Later in their education, students may encounter more sophisticated words, such as *speculate, prospect, perspective,* and *conspicuous.*

Spanish cognates: *el espectador* (the male spectator), *inspeccionar* (to inspect), *el respeto* (the respect)

Teachable moments: One of any school's most important words is *respect.* Consider how this word derives its meaning: to look (*spect-*) back upon (*re-*). It might give your class insight into how to show respect to others if they think of respect as a form of *looking back* at someone, as opposed to the disrespect shown by self-absorption and distractedness.

34. Latin word: *struere*
    Means: to build
    Inside the words, it takes these forms: *stru-*
    Examples: *structure, instruct, destroy, destruction, construct/ construction/constructive instrument*

Later in their education, students might encounter more sophisticated words, such as *construe, misconstrue, restructure,* and *infrastructure.*

Spanish Cognates: *la estructura* (the structure), *instruir* (to instruct), *destruir* (to destroy), *construir* (to construct), *la construcción* (the construction), *el instrumento* (the instrument)

Teachable moments: Etymologically, the words *education/educator* and *instruct/instructor* have complementary meanings: an educator leads, or draws out, that which is within the student, while an instructor builds knowledge into a student.

35. Latin word: *tenere* and *tendere*
    Means: to hold (*tenere*) and to stretch (*tendere*)

Inside the words, it takes these forms: *ten-, tend-, -tain, tin-*
Examples: *contain, retain/retention, detain/detention, tenant, obtain,
pertain, sustain, maintain, entertain, lieutenant, continue, intend/intent/
intention, tendon, attend, pretend, tent*

Later in their education, students may encounter more sophisticated words,
such as *tenure, ascertain, tendon, tendril, attenuate, tenet,* and *tenuous.*

Spanish cognates: *contener* (to contain), *retener* (to retain), *detener* (to
detain), *la detención* (the detention), *el teniente* (the lieutenant), *obtener*
(to obtain), *sustener* (to sustain), *mantener* (to maintain), *entretener* (to
entertain), *continuar* (to continue), *el intento* (the attempt)

Teachable moments: We're considering these two words together because
they are so close in meaning. This large word family exemplifies how a
native Spanish speaker, just by knowing one of the most common of Spanish
words (*tener,* to have or hold), can access multiple Tier II English words and
their forms.

36. Latin word: *tractare*
    Means: to drag or draw
    Inside the words, it takes these forms: *tract-*
    Examples: *tractor, traction, subtract, attract, detract, distract, retract,
    extract, contract, abstract*

Later in their education, students may encounter more sophisticated words,
such as *tractable, intractable, protractor,* and *protracted.*

Spanish cognates: *el tractor* (the tractor), *atraer* (to attract), *extraer* (to
extract), *el contracto* (the contract), *el abstracto* (the abstract)

Teachable moments: The way this root shows up in words is particularly
systematic. Its forms are predictable and easy to see, and it recruits most of
the common prefixes. For this reason, it might make a good starting point
for teaching about word components.

37. Latin word: *vertere*
    Means: to turn
    Inside the words, it takes these forms: *vert-, vers-*
    Examples: *converse/conversation, versatile, revert/reverse, invert/inversion,
    convert/conversion, adversary, controversy, divert/diversion, verse*

Later in their education, students may encounter more sophisticated words, such as *avert/aversion, subversive, transversal.*

> Spanish cognates: *conversar* (converse), *converso* (convert), *conversación* (conversation), *revés* (reverse), *invertir* (invert), *inversión* (inversion), *convertir* (convert), *conversión* (conversion), *controversia* (controversy), *diversión* (diversion), *verso* (verse)

Teachable moments: We get insight about the turn-taking nature of a conversation when we consider its etymology. A bit more puzzling is the connection between turns and verse, as in the verses of poetry and songs, but we can see "turns" of meaning in that each verse coheres around a theme or subject, which alters with each verse.

> 38. Latin word: *verbum*
>   Means: word
>   Inside the words, it takes these forms: *verb-*
>   Examples: *verb, proverb, verbal, nonverbal*

Later in their education, students may encounter more sophisticated words, such as *proverbial, verbalize, verbatim,* and *verbose.*

> Spanish cognates: *la expresión* (the expression), *verbal* (verbal)

Teachable moments: Proverbs themselves are teachable moments because they employ symbolism to tell a larger truth. We may be referring to proverbs as *sayings*, which is fine in the early stages of the concept, and offers the teachable moments of transitioning the word *sayings* into the word *proverbs*. If you do that naturally, just substituting *proverbs* for *sayings*, you will soon find that students make that transition as well.

> 39. Latin word: *videre*
>   Means: to see
>   Inside the words, it takes these forms: *vic-, vid-, vie-, vis-*
>   Examples: *television, video, view, vision, visit, visor, advice, advise, evidence, improvise, interview, review/revision, provide/provision, visible, supervise, survey*

Later in their education, students may encounter more sophisticated words, such as *surveillance, visionary, purvey, vista, visa, proviso,* and *provisional.*

Spanish cognates: *la televisión* (the television), *la vista* (the sight, i.e., vision), *visitar* (to visit), *la visita* (the visit), *el aviso* (the notice), *la evidencia* (the evidence), *la revista* (the magazine), *visible* (visible)

Teachable moments: The word *video* is actually Latin for *I see.* This is another good starting point for the study of etymology because so many of the words deriving from this root are familiar.

40. Latin word: *vocare*
     Means: to call
     Inside the words, it takes these forms: *vok-, voc-*
     Examples: *vocal, vocabulary, provoke/provocation; revoke/evocation; advocate*

Later in their education, students may encounter more sophisticated words, such as: *vocation, avocation, invoke/invocation,* and *evoke/evocative.*

Spanish cognates: *vocabulario* (the vocabulary)

Teachable moments: Notice the spelling opportunity in that the verb forms *provoke, invoke,* and *evoke* use the *k,* which converts to a *c* in the noun forms *provocation, invocation,* and *evocative.*